FAITH CLINIC

VOLUME XXII

- UNFORGIVENESS EDITION -

I FORGAVE THEM.. I JUST REHEARSE THE CONVERSATION DAILY

DR. PATRICIA S. TANNER

IBG Publications, Inc.

Published by I.B.G. Publications, Inc., a Power to Wealth Company

Web address: www.ibgpublications.com

admin@ibgpublications.com / 904-419-9810

Copyright, 2026 by Patricia S. Tanner

IBG Publications, Inc., Jacksonville, FL

ISBN: 978-1-971850-06-1

Tanner, Patricia S.
Faith Clinic, Volume XXII- Unforgiveness Edition-I Forgave Them… I Just Rehearse The Conversation Daily

Printed in the United States of America.

DEDICATION

To the ones who tried to forgive but still feel the ache.

To those who pray for people they secretly still argue with in their minds.

To the hearts that were wounded deeply, smiled politely, and said, "I'm fine," while replaying the moment repeatedly.

This book is dedicated to you.

May you find the courage to release what keeps replaying.
May you choose freedom over familiar pain.
And may God heal the places that forgiveness alone could not reach.

With compassion and conviction,

DR. PATRICIA S. TANNER
The Faith Doctor

TABLE OF CONTENTS

📖 FAITH CLINIC INTAKE FORM

Patient Name: _______________________________

Date:___________________

Attending Physician: The Holy Spirit (Chief of Heart Surgery)

Reason for Visit:" I said I forgave them, but my peace didn't get the memo."

🔍 CHIEF COMPLAINT

(Please check all that apply)

☐ I replay conversations that already happened

☐ I imagine conversations that will never happen

☐ I get emotional reactions from things that shouldn't matter anymore

☐ I feel spiritually mature but emotionally irritated

☐ I flinch when certain names are mentioned

☐ I say "I'm fine" quickly and aggressively

☐ I feel justified, not healed

☐ I've prayed about it… repeatedly… with the same outcome

☐ I'm tired of carrying this, but scared to put it down

🧠 SYMPTOM HISTORY

How long have you been experiencing these symptoms?

☐ Weeks

☐ Months

☐ Years

☐ Long enough that it feels normal

When symptoms flare up, what usually triggers them?
☐ Seeing the person
☐ Hearing about the person
☐ Remembering what was said
☐ Remembering what was *never* said
☐ Being misunderstood
☐ Being reminded that they "moved on"
☐ Being told to "just forgive"

℞ OFFENSE DETAILS

(You don't have to relive everything—just tell the truth)
Who hurt you?
☐ Family
☐ Friend
☐ Church leader
☐ Romantic partner
☐ Authority figure
☐ Someone who never apologized
☐ Someone who apologized badly

What hurt the most? *(Check the closest answer)*
☐ Betrayal
☐ Abandonment
☐ Public humiliation
☐ Gaslighting
☐ Being misunderstood
☐ Being replaced
☐ Being silenced
☐ Being blamed for someone else's behavior

What still feels unresolved?

INTERNAL RESPONSE ASSESSMENT

(Be honest. This form is confidential.)
When I think about the offense, my body reacts with:
☐ Tight chest
☐ Jaw clenching
☐ Shoulder tension
☐ Sudden fatigue
☐ Anger disguised as calm
☐ Sadness disguised as strength
☐ A strong urge to explain myself (again)

📖 SPIRITUAL HISTORY (RELEVANT TO CURRENT CONDITION)

☐ I was taught forgiveness means "don't feel it anymore"
☐ I was taught forgiveness means "restore access immediately"
☐ I was taught forgiveness means "God will be disappointed if I'm honest"
☐ I confuse forgiveness with pretending
☐ I confuse boundaries with bitterness
☐ I confuse silence with peace

📃 CURRENT COPING METHODS

(Please check what you've tried)
☐ Prayer without processing
☐ Scripture without honesty
☐ Journaling but avoiding the hard parts
☐ Over-functioning to prove I'm fine
☐ Avoidance disguised as wisdom
☐ Emotional numbing

☐ Humor to deflect pain
☐ Spiritual language to shut down feelings

⚠ WARNING SIGNS (CLINICAL OBSERVATION)

☐ You feel righteous but not restful
☐ You're guarded, not healed
☐ You're calm, but not free
☐ You've learned how to survive the pain, not release it
☐ You're managing the wound instead of letting God heal it

✎ PRELIMINARY DIAGNOSIS

(To be confirmed during treatment)
☐ Chronic Unforgiveness
☐ Emotional Rehearsal Syndrome
☐ Delayed Grief Response
☐ Spiritual Bypassing
☐ Nervous System Hypervigilance
☐ Boundary Confusion Disorder

📝 PATIENT ACKNOWLEDGMENT

Please implement the following statements:

______ I acknowledge that forgiveness is a process, not a performance.

______ I understand that healing may be uncomfortable before it is peaceful.

______ I agree to stop pretending I'm over something I haven't processed.

______ I consent to truth, not just relief.

_____ I understand that letting go does not mean what happened was okay.

Patient Signature: ________________________________

Date: ________________________

🕊 CLINIC NOTE (FOR PATIENT REVIEW)

You are not here because you're bitter. You are here because something mattered—and it was mishandled. Healing begins when honesty replaces rehearsal.

🏥 FAITH CLINIC ID WRISTBAND

This wristband is not decorative. It is a reminder. You are in treatment.

📋 PATIENT IDENTIFICATION

Patient Name: ________________________________

Clinic ID #: FC-UF-___________

Edition: Unforgiveness

Status: Under Active Treatment

Admitted For: Chronic Emotional Rehearsal

Primary Physician: The Holy Spirit

🩺 DIAGNOSIS (PRIMARY)

☑ **Unforgiveness**
☑ Emotional Rehearsal Syndrome
☑ Delayed Grief Response

☑ Nervous System Hypervigilance
☑ Boundary Confusion

⚠ ALLERGY ALERTS

(Exposure may cause relapses)
🚫 Spiritual Bypassing
🚫 "Just forgive and move on" advice
🚫 Minimizing your pain to sound mature
🚫 Forced reconciliation
🚫 Fake peace
🚫 Silence disguised as strength

🧠 CURRENT SYMPTOMS

(May fluctuate during treatment)
• Mental replay of unresolved conversations
• Emotional reactions without warning
• Irritation disguised as calm
• Hyper-awareness around specific names, places, or memories
• Fatigue from carrying what should have been released

VITAL REMINDERS

(Read daily or when triggered)
✓ Forgiveness is not denial
✓ Forgiveness is not access
✓ Forgiveness does not mean it didn't hurt
✓ Forgiveness is releasing the right to rehearse
✓ Healing can be quiet and still real

🚨 EMERGENCY PROTOCOL

If patient begins replaying the offense:

1. Pause. Do not engage the script.
2. Name the feeling without judging it.
3. Remind yourself: *"I am safe now."*
4. Redirect attention to present reality.
5. Pray honestly — not politely.

📖 SCRIPTURAL STABILIZER

(For moments of emotional flare-up)
"Forget the former things; do not dwell on the past. See, I am doing a new thing." — Isaiah 43:18–19

🕊 CONSENT TO TREATMENT

☐ I consent to healing even if it's uncomfortable
☐ I agree to stop rehearsing what I cannot change
☐ I release the offense without excusing it
☐ I choose peace over control
☐ I understand healing is a process, not a moment
Patient Initials: ___________
Date: ___________

📝 CLINIC NOTE (NON-NEGOTIABLE TRUTH)

This wristband does not mean you are weak. It means you are honest. You are not being punished — you are being healed.

PERSONAL NOTES

Welcome To The Faith Clinic

Unforgiveness Edition

Welcome to the Faith Clinic.

Not the kind with fluorescent lights, awkward clipboards, and someone calling your name wrong, but the kind where honesty is finally allowed to breathe. The kind where you don't have to pretend you're healed just because you know the right verses. The kind where we stop asking you to be spiritually impressive and start helping you be emotionally free.

You didn't arrive here because you're failing at forgiveness. You arrived here because you've been trying to do it *alone*, quietly, and politely, while carrying pain that was never meant to be managed in silence. In this clinic, we don't rush you, shame you, or pressure you to "move on." We assess. We listen. We treat what's happening, not what looks good on the outside.

Here's what you need to know as you walk in: unforgiveness is not a moral defect. It's not proof that you're immature, rebellious, or spiritually stubborn. Most of the time, it's proof that something hurt deeply and never got resolved safely. It's what happens when pain is real, but closure is incomplete. When your faith says one thing, but your body never felt safe enough to agree.

In many faith spaces, unforgiveness gets reduced to command instead of understood as a condition. You're told to forgive quickly, quietly, and completely, often without being given the space to grieve what was lost, violated, or taken from you. You're expected to release the offense while your nervous system is still bracing for impact. And when that doesn't work, the conclusion is usually the same: *you must not be trying hard enough.*

That narrative ends here.

The Faith Clinic exists because healing requires structure, safety, and truth, not pressure. Just like physical wounds don't heal because you demand they do, emotional wounds don't heal because you quote scripture at them aggressively. They heal when they're acknowledged, tended to, and given time to close properly. Forgiveness works the same way.

Inside this clinic, we treat unforgiveness the way it shows up, not as rage or revenge fantasies, but as rehearsals. As looping thoughts. As emotional reactions that feel disproportionate but won't go away. As a body that tightens when certain names are mentioned. As exhaustion from carrying a story you're tired of telling but haven't been able to put down.

Here, we don't confuse forgiveness with forgetting. We don't confuse boundaries with bitterness. And we don't confuse silence with peace.

You'll notice this clinic runs a little differently. Instead of sermons, you'll find assessments. Instead of guilt, you'll find clarity. Instead of pressure to reconcile, you'll find permission to heal without reopening wounds. Instead of vague encouragement, you'll find tools, because feelings fluctuate, but systems stabilize.

You are not here to prove how holy you are. You are here to get well.

That means we will ask honest questions. We will name patterns you may have normalized. We will slow down moments you've been rushing past. And at times, we will gently confront the stories you've been using to survive that are now keeping you stuck. Not to shame you, but to free you.

Healing in this clinic is not measured by how quickly you stop feeling things. It's measured by how quickly your body recovers when feelings show up. Progress is not silence. Progress is regulation. Progress is choosing not to rehearse even when the memory knocks. Progress is peace returning faster than it used to.

And let's be clear: forgiveness here is not about letting anyone off the hook. It's about taking *yourself* off the emotional cross of carrying something that keeps reopening you. Forgiveness in this clinic is not denial, tolerance, or access. It is release. It is choosing to stop bleeding from a wound you didn't cause but are ready to heal.

You are allowed to take your time here. Clinics don't rush patients. Some chapters may feel lighter. Others may hit places you've been avoiding for years. That doesn't mean you're doing it wrong, it usually means you've finally hit the right spot.

So, take a breath. Drop your shoulders. Unclench your jaw.

You are safe here.
You are not behind.
You are not weak for needing help.

Welcome to the Faith Clinic.
Treatment begins with honesty.

18

INTRODUCTION

I Forgave Them… I Just Rehearse the Conversation Daily

You probably didn't pick up this book because you're bitter. Bitter people don't usually buy books about forgiveness. They buy wine, distractions, new boundaries with zero explanation, or spiritual language that helps them sound healed without being healed. You picked up this book because you are tired. Tired of thinking about something you said you were done with. Tired of replaying conversations that ended years ago but still feel unfinished. Tired of being spiritually aware enough to know you *should* be over it, yet human enough to realize you're not.

You forgave them. You really did. At least, you meant to. You prayed the prayer. You released the words. You even said it out loud so God could hear you clearly. But somehow, forgiveness didn't shut your mind off. It didn't stop your body from tightening when their name comes up. It didn't stop your chest from getting heavy when something reminds you of what happened. And it didn't stop you from rehearsing what you *wish* you had said, what you *should* have said, or what you're still secretly hoping you'll get the chance to say one day.

This book exists because that experience is far more common than anyone wants to admit, especially in faith spaces. In church, unforgiveness is treated like a character flaw instead of a wound. It's something you're supposed to confess quickly, repent immediately, and move past quietly. The problem is, wounds don't respond to pressure. They respond to care. And when forgiveness is rushed, forced, or performed instead of processed, it doesn't heal you, it just teaches you how to pretend better.

The Faith Clinic was never designed for people who don't believe in forgiveness. It was designed for people who believe in it deeply but feel like it keeps slipping through their fingers. People who love God but feel confused when their faith says "peace" and their nervous system says "danger." People who are emotionally intelligent enough to name their pain but spiritually mature enough to want real healing—not just relief, not just silence, and not just a good public testimony that privately falls apart at night.

Unforgiveness is sneaky like that. It doesn't always show up as rage or revenge. Most of the time, it shows up as rehearsal. As mental looping. As quiet resentment that sounds like logic. As "I'm fine" said a little too quickly. As emotional distance disguised as wisdom. As boundaries that aren't boundaries, but emotional barricades built out of exhaustion and self-protection. You tell yourself you're guarding your heart, but if you're honest, it feels more like you're guarding a crime scene that never fully closed.

What makes unforgiveness especially exhausting is that it convinces you you're doing something productive. Replaying the conversation feels like processing. Rehashing the details feels like clarity. Imagining how you'd explain yourself *now* feels empowering. But none of it moves you forward. It just keeps you emotionally tethered to a moment that already took enough from you. Unforgiveness isn't loud; it's repetitive. It doesn't scream; it whispers the same script again until it feels familiar enough to mistake for truth.

This book is not here to shame you for that. It's here to name it.

The Faith Clinic approach is different because it refuses to treat emotional pain as a spiritual inconvenience. It doesn't ask you to minimize what hurt you to prove your faith. It doesn't confuse forgiveness with access or healing with silence. And it doesn't rush you to reconciliation before your body even feels safe. Instead, it treats unforgiveness like what it is: a condition that develops when pain is real, resolution is incomplete, and the nervous system never got the memo that the danger has passed.

That's why this book is structured like a clinic instead of a sermon. Clinics don't shame patients for symptoms. They assess them. They don't demand instant recovery. They create treatment plans. They don't confuse compliance with healing. They look for patterns, triggers, and progress over time. And most importantly, they understand that just because something is invisible doesn't mean it isn't affecting the entire system.

You'll notice quickly that this book doesn't rush you into forgiveness language. That's intentional. Too many people already know *what* forgiveness is supposed to be, but very few have been taught *how* it works, especially when the hurt was deep, the apology never came, or the relationship never recovered. Forgiveness is not a switch you flip; it's a process your body has to learn. And until your body feels safe, your mind will keep rehearsing. Not because you're failing, but because something in you is still trying to protect you.

Throughout these chapters, we will talk honestly about why you keep replaying the moment, why "moving on" hasn't worked, and why your faith hasn't failed you just because your feelings haven't caught up yet. We'll unpack the difference between forgiveness and reconciliation, between boundaries and bitterness, between peace and emotional numbness. We'll talk about the grief that often hides underneath unforgiveness, the grief of not being heard, not being protected, not being believed, or not being chosen.

You'll also notice that this book doesn't demand closure. That's because closure is overrated. Closure requires cooperation from people who may never be safe, self-aware, or accountable enough to give it. Healing, on the other hand, does not require their participation. It requires yours. And more importantly, it requires honesty, the kind that stops pretending you're over something just because you're tired of carrying it.

This is where the tools come in. The Intake Form, the ID Wristband, the Emergency Wallet Card, the Doctor's Orders, the 30-Day Treatment Plan, and the Monthly Progress Tracker aren't gimmicks. They are structure for moments when emotions hijack logic and faith needs support. They exist because healing doesn't happen in abstract ideas; it happens in daily interruptions, repeated choices, and compassionate awareness. They help you measure progress not by whether the memory disappears, but by how quickly peace returns when it shows up.

One of the most important truths you'll encounter in this book is this: healing is not the absence of memory; it is the absence of emotional bleeding. You may never forget what happened. You may never agree with how it was handled. You may never get the apology, explanation, or accountability you deserved. But you can reach a place where the memory no longer controls your body, your reactions, or your sense of safety. You can reach a place where the story no longer demands rehearsal to feel relevant.

That doesn't make you weak. It makes you free.

This book is for the person who is spiritually sincere but emotionally exhausted. The one who loves deeply, forgives often, and still wonders why some wounds linger longer than others. It's for the person who has done everything "right" and still feels unsettled. The one who is tired of being told to forgive when what they really need is permission to heal.

As you move through these chapters, you may feel exposed. You may feel seen. You may feel defensive at times, and relieved at others. That's normal. Healing always disrupts the stories we've been using to survive. But if you stay with the process, if you let yourself be honest instead of impressive, you will begin to notice something subtle but powerful. The rehearsals will shorten. The emotional charge will soften. The urge to explain will fade. And peace, real peace, will stop feeling like something you have to force.

You don't have to rush through this book. Clinics don't rush patients through treatment. Take the chapters at your pace. Use the tools. Revisit the sections that sting a little more than others. That's usually where the healing is working. And remember: forgiveness is not something you perform to prove your faith. It is something you practice to protect your peace.

You are not behind. You are not broken. You are not failing God because you're still affected by what hurt you. You are human, you were wounded, and you are allowed to heal properly.

Welcome to the Faith Clinic.
Please state the offense.

Chapter 1
Welcome To The Faith Clinic: Please State The Offense

You don't walk into a clinic unless something hurts. People who feel fine don't fill out intake forms. They don't sit in waiting rooms. They don't quietly admit, *"I think something is wrong, but I can't explain it."* You don't open a book like this because life is peaceful and uncomplicated. You open it because there is a tension you can't shake, something unresolved that keeps tapping you on the shoulder no matter how busy, spiritual, or productive you try to be.

So before we go any further, let's get something clear: your presence here already tells the truth. Something hurt. Something stayed. Something didn't heal the way you thought it would.

The Faith Clinic doesn't begin with instructions. It begins with assessment. Not because we want to dwell on the past, but because untreated wounds don't disappear, they adapt. They show up later as anxiety, irritability, emotional withdrawal, spiritual exhaustion, or a constant low-grade defensiveness you can't quite name. And unforgiveness, contrary to popular belief, doesn't always look like rage. Most of the time, it looks like composure with a pulse underneath it.

This chapter is not about fixing anything yet. It's about naming. Because you cannot heal what you refuse to acknowledge, and you cannot release what you keep pretending doesn't matter anymore.

In traditional faith environments, "state the offense" is often skipped. You're encouraged to jump straight to forgiveness language before your body has even processed what happened. You're told to pray it away, release it, give it to God, and move on. While those phrases sound spiritual, they often bypass the most critical step of healing: telling the truth without rushing to clean it up.

In this clinic, we slow that process down.

When a patient arrives with physical pain, no competent doctor responds by saying, "Well, you shouldn't feel that way." They ask where it hurts. They ask how long it's been hurting. They ask what makes it worse and what makes it better. They listen before they prescribe. Emotional and spiritual healing deserves the same respect.

So, let's begin there.

The offense may not be dramatic. It may not even sound "bad enough" when you say it out loud. It could have been a moment you were dismissed, overlooked, misunderstood, or spoken over. It could have been a betrayal that no one else saw coming. It could have been a slow erosion of trust rather than a single explosive event. What matters is not how it compares to someone else's pain. What matters is that it marked you, and your system remembers.

One of the biggest lies surrounding unforgiveness is that if something still affects you, you must not have forgiven "correctly." That lie keeps people stuck in cycles of shame and self-blame instead of healing. Forgiveness is not a spiritual eraser. It is a release process, and release happens in layers, especially when the wound involves power, attachment, abandonment, or identity.

Many people forgive with their mouth long before their nervous system ever gets the memo.

That's why you can genuinely mean it when you say, "I forgive them," and still feel a jolt in your body when their name comes up. That's why you can love God deeply and still find yourself replaying conversations at night. That's why you can be emotionally intelligent, spiritually mature, and still triggered by things you thought you were done with.

None of that means you failed. It means the offense is never fully closed.

This chapter invites you to stop rushing past that truth.

When we say, "State the offense," we are not asking you to relive trauma or reopen wounds recklessly. We are asking you to identify what your body already knows. To give language to what has been living under the surface so healing can become intentional instead of accidental.

For many readers, this is uncomfortable. Naming the offense feels like going backward. You may worry that acknowledging it will make it stronger, or that God will be disappointed that you're still affected. But avoidance doesn't weaken pain, it just makes it quieter and more persistent. Suppressed wounds don't heal; they wait.

You may also notice resistance rising as you read this chapter. Thoughts like, *"It wasn't that bad," "Other people had it worse," "I should be over this by now,"* or *"I don't want to give this any more attention."* Those thoughts are not signs of strength. They are signs of self-protection. And while self-protection once helped you survive, it may now be interfering with your ability to heal.

The Faith Clinic does not judge resistance. We expect it. Resistance usually shows up when healing threatens a coping mechanism you've relied on for a long time. If you learned to minimize pain to keep relationships, to stay safe, or to survive spiritually, honesty can feel dangerous. That doesn't mean it is. It means your system needs reassurance before it can let go.

So, let's be clear: stating the offense is not about blaming. It's about clarity. It's about separating what happened from who you are. When offenses go unnamed, they tend to fuse with identity. You don't just remember what happened, you become the one it happened to. And that identity quietly shapes your reactions, boundaries, expectations, and relationships long after the event is over. Naming the offense begins the process of disentangling yourself from it.

As you move through this chapter, you may realize that what you've 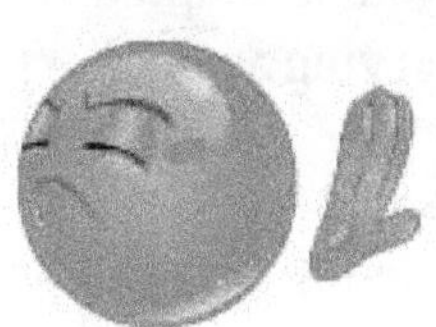 been calling "unforgiveness" is unresolved grief. Grief for what you thought would be different. Grief for how you expected to be treated. Grief for the version of yourself that trusted freely before the injury. Forgiveness without grief often turns into numbness or resentment because something essential was skipped.

This clinic does not skip steps.

We also need to address something important early on: forgiveness is not synonymous with reconciliation. Stating the offense does not obligate you to restore access to people who were unsafe, dismissive, or harmful. Healing does not require you to minimize boundaries. In fact, boundaries often become clearer *after* forgiveness begins, not before.

Too many people delay healing because they believe forgiveness means reopening doors they worked hard to close. That belief creates an internal stalemate: part of you wants peace, and part of you refuses to sacrifice safety for it. Until that conflict is addressed, unforgiveness remains a form of protection, not rebellion.

This chapter sets the groundwork for resolving that conflict.

As you state the offense, whether on paper, in prayer, or quietly in your own awareness, pay attention to what happens in your body. Do you tense? Do you feel heavy? Do you want to rush past it? Those reactions are data. They are not weakness. They are clues pointing toward where healing needs to focus.

You are not here to perform forgiveness. You are here to experience it.

That means we are going to take this seriously. We are going to give language to things you may have dismissed for years. We are going to stop pretending that spiritual maturity means emotional amnesia. And we are going to respect the fact that your system adapted for a reason, even if those adaptations are no longer serving you.

This chapter does not demand answers. It invites honesty.

Before you move on, pause and consider this question, not to answer perfectly, but to answer truthfully: *What moment does my mind keep returning to, even though I say I'm over it?* That moment is not random. It is asking for attention, not rehearsal. Healing begins when you listen instead of looping.

In the Faith Clinic, stating the offense is not about staying stuck. It is about finally giving yourself permission to stop carrying  something you were never meant to manage indefinitely. It is the first act of courage in a process that prioritizes peace over performance.

You are not behind for being here. You are right on time.

Welcome to treatment.

💊 Faith Prescription

Stabilization Before Healing

Before forgiveness becomes a practice, it must first become a safe process. The goal of this prescription is not to fix anything yet. It is to stop the emotional bleeding that happens when wounds are ignored, minimized, or rushed past in the name of spirituality.

For the next phase of your healing, your only responsibility is honesty without urgency.

This means you are not required to:

- Feel peace yet

- Resolve the offense yet

- Understand everything yet

- Forgive perfectly yet

Your assignment is simpler, and harder. You are to notice without rehearsing.

When the memory surfaces, you do not engage it. You do not argue with it. You do not correct it. You do not spiritualize it away. You simply acknowledge: *"This is the offense. This is the place that still hurts."*

This prescription may feel passive, but it is not. It is active restraint. It is choosing not to reopen a wound just because it knocks. It is allowing awareness to replace autopilot. It is learning how to sit with truth without demanding immediate relief.

For this stage of treatment:

- Speak honestly to God, not impressively

- Name the offense without narrating it

- Stop correcting yourself for still being affected

Healing cannot begin until you stop punishing yourself for having symptoms.

Prescription Duration: Ongoing
Reassessment: End of Chapter 2

🧬 Spiritual Vitamin: Truth That Nourishes The Process

"The Lord is close to the brokenhearted and saves those who are crushed in spirit."
— **Psalm 34:18**

This verse is not a command. It is a positioning statement.

God does not stand at a distance waiting for you to get over it. He draws closer when something in you is crushed, fractured, or overwhelmed. That means your honesty does not repel Him, it attracts Him. Your awareness does not disappoint Him, it invites His nearness.

Read that again carefully. God is not waiting for you to forgive before He comes close. He comes close because something hurt.

Let this truth nourish you during this phase: you do not have to resolve the offense to be held by God. You only must stop pretending it didn't matter.

🕊 Holy Spirit Consult: Discernment, Not Condemnation

Take a moment and sit quietly with this question. Do not rush it. Do not analyze it. Just let it surface gently.

Holy Spirit, what am I afraid will happen if I fully acknowledge this offense?

You may hear fear of:
- Losing spiritual credibility.
- Becoming bitter.
- Reopening pain.

- Having to confront something you avoided.
- Realizing how deeply it hurt.

Whatever rises is not something to correct. It is something to notice.

The Holy Spirit does not expose wounds to shame you. He exposes them to heal you. And He will never demand speed where safety is required.

If nothing comes up, that's okay. Sometimes awareness comes slowly. Sometimes your system needs repetition before it trusts the process. There is no failure here, only pacing.

🙏 Guided Prayer: Honest, Not Polished

"God, I'm here because something still hurts.
I've tried to move on.
I've tried to forgive quickly.
I've tried to be strong and spiritual about it.

But the truth is, something stayed.

I don't want to rehearse this anymore.
I don't want to carry it quietly either.
I don't know what healing looks like yet,
but I want it to be real.

Help me tell the truth without rushing myself.
Help me trust that You are close, not disappointed.
Help me believe that honesty is not rebellion.

I place this offense in Your presence—not to solve it,
but to stop carrying it alone.

Amen."

📝 Journal Reflection Page: Intake-Level Honesty

Do not overthink these prompts. Write what comes naturally. Short or long responses are both acceptable. This is not about eloquence. It is about accuracy.

1. The moment I keep returning to, even though I say I'm over it, is:

____

____

____

____

____

2. When I think about this offense, my body reacts by:

____

____

____

____

____

____

____

3. The emotion I feel most when this comes up is:

☐ Anger ☐ Sadness ☐ Confusion ☐ Shame ☐ Fear ☐ Grief

☐ Numbness

4. What I needed in that moment but didn't receive was:

____

____

____

5. One sentence of truth I can hold this week is: *"I am allowed to heal without rushing."*

📖 Clinic Note: Read Before Moving On

✓ You have not failed forgiveness.
✓ You have not disappointed God.
✓ You have not regressed.
✓ You have simply arrived at the place where healing begins.

This chapter was not about letting go.
It was about setting the wound down gently instead of carrying it tighter.

Treatment is underway.

When you are ready, proceed to Chapter 2: ***The Symptom You Keep Ignoring: Replaying What You'll Never Say***

We will go slowly.
We will go honestly.
And we will not leave you exposed without support.

DR. PATRICIA S. TANNER

PERSONAL NOTES

Chapter 2

The Symptom You Keep Ignoring: Replaying What You'll Never Say

The replay rarely announces itself. It doesn't show up as a dramatic breakdown or a loud emotional outburst. Most of the time, it slips in quietly, while you're driving, folding laundry, brushing your teeth, lying in bed at night, or sitting in a room where your body is present, but your mind has time traveled. One second, you're fine. The next, you're back there. Back in the moment where you were interrupted, dismissed, betrayed, misunderstood, or silenced. And suddenly, you're saying everything you didn't say then, only now, no one is listening.

This is the symptom most people ignore because it feels harmless. After all, you're not yelling. You're not confronting anyone. You're not acting out. You're just thinking. Quietly. Internally. Rehearsing.

But make no mistake: replaying what you'll never say is not neutral. It is not "just processing." It is not wisdom. It is not discernment. It is your nervous system stuck in an unresolved loop, trying to complete something that never reached safety or closure. And the reason it's exhausting is because your body doesn't know the difference between a real conversation and a vividly imagined one. Every replay costs your energy. Every rehearsal reactivates the wound.

This chapter is about naming that loop, not to shame you, but to free you from mistaking it for healing.

Many people believe that if they keep replaying the moment, eventually it will lose its power. That if they just think it through one more time, they'll finally understand what went wrong, how they should have responded, or what it all meant. But the truth is, rehearsals don't bring resolution. They bring reinforcement. Each time you replay the conversation, you strengthen the neural pathway associated with it. You teach your brain, *This is important. Keep this accessible. Stay alert.*

So, the replay doesn't fade. It deepens.

What makes this symptom especially deceptive is that it often feels justified. You're not fantasizing about revenge. You're clarifying. You're correcting the record. You're finally standing up for yourself—just privately. You tell yourself you're preparing in case it ever comes up again. You're rehearsing for wisdom. You're making sure you'll never be caught off guard like that again.

But if we're honest, most of these conversations will never happen. The person may never ask. They may never listen. They may never care. Or they may no longer be in your life at all. And yet, you keep talking to them in your head as if the moment is still open, as if the door is still ajar, as if closure is one perfectly worded sentence away.

That is not preparation. That is attachment.

Replaying conversations is one of the most common manifestations of unresolved unforgiveness, not because you want to stay angry, but because something inside you doesn't feel settled. The offense may be old, but the emotional charge is not. And until your system feels safe, it will keep pulling the memory forward, asking you to finish what was interrupted.

This is where many faith-driven people get confused. You've forgiven. You've prayed. You've released them 'to God.' So, why is your mind still doing this? Because forgiveness spoken does not automatically equal forgiveness embodied.

You can forgive with your beliefs long before your body agrees. And when the body doesn't agree, it tries to protect you the only way it knows how: by rehearsing. By staying vigilant. By keeping the story alive in case it needs to defend you again.

Rehearsal is a form of self-protection. It is your system saying, *"I don't want to be unprepared if this happens again."* The problem is that protection outlives the threat. The danger may be gone, but the body doesn't know that yet. So, it keeps practicing, just in case.

That's why you can feel spiritually at peace and still mentally on  edge. That's why you can say you're healed and still feel a rush of adrenaline when something reminds you of the offense. That's why you can genuinely wish the person well and still feel irritated when their name comes up. Your faith moved forward. Your nervous system didn't.

And no one taught you how to bring them back into alignment.

In church culture, this symptom often gets mislabeled as a lack of forgiveness or a lack of faith. But labeling it that way only adds shame to the loop. Now you're not just replaying the conversation, you're also judging yourself for replaying it. You tell yourself you should be further along. You question your maturity. You wonder why God hasn't "taken this away yet." And the shame tightens the loop even more.

The Faith Clinic approach is different. We don't ask, *"Why haven't you forgiven?"* We ask, *"Why does your system still feel unsafe?"*

Because when you replay a conversation, your body is not trying to be sinful. It's trying to be prepared.

Think about the last time the replay showed up. Pay attention to what came before it. Was it a moment of vulnerability? A reminder of being dismissed? A situation where you felt powerless, misunderstood, or overlooked again? Replays are rarely random. They are triggered by present-day experiences that echo the original wound. That's important to understand, because it means the replay is not about the past alone. It's about the present moment touching an old injury.

For example, you may replay a conversation with a parent after feeling unheard by a friend. You may rehearse something you wish you had said to a former partner after being dismissed at work. You may mentally confront a church leader from years ago after hearing a sermon that minimizes pain. The mind reaches for familiar territory. The nervous system recognizes the pattern and says, *"We've been here before."*

And suddenly, you're back in the room where it all started.

This is why telling yourself to "just stop thinking about it" never works. The replay is not a problem with thought. It's a safety problem. And safety cannot be commanded; it must be restored.

Another reason this symptom persists is because many people confuse silence with resolution. Just because you didn't speak up doesn't mean the issue closed. Just because time passed doesn't mean your system processed what happened. Silence often freezes a moment instead of resolving it. And frozen moments demand attention later.

This is especially true if the offense involved power imbalance, when you couldn't speak freely because it wasn't safe, appropriate, or allowed. Children, employees, church members, spouses in controlling dynamics, many people learned early on that speaking up came with consequences. So, they swallowed words in the moment, and those words lodged themselves in the body instead.

Years later, they're still trying to get out.

Replaying the conversation is the mind's attempt to give voice to what was silenced. It's the body saying, *"I didn't get to finish."* And until that is acknowledged, the replay will keep returning, not because you're holding a grudge, but because something in you wants to be heard.

This is where forgiveness gets misunderstood again. Forgiveness does not mean you never get to name what happened. Forgiveness does not mean you pretend it didn't affect you. Forgiveness does not mean you silence yourself internally just because the external conversation is over. In fact, true forgiveness often begins *after* you stop rehearsing and start acknowledging. The replay loses power when it is recognized for what it is: a symptom, not a strategy.

And here's the part most people don't expect, replaying conversations can delay forgiveness. Not because you're unwilling, but because rehearsal keeps the emotional charge alive. Every imagined sentence reactivates the same chemicals, the same tension, the same posture. You are, quite literally, reliving the offense in your body repeatedly. Healing cannot settle into a system that keeps reopening itself. This is why peace feels so elusive. You're not refusing to let go. You're practicing the injury.

The goal of this chapter is not to shame you for that. It's to help you see it clearly so you can interrupt it gently. Not by forcing silence, but by offering your system something safer than rehearsal.

As we move forward in this book, you will learn how to interrupt the replay without suppressing truth. How to acknowledge the offense without narrating it endlessly. How to allow the emotion without reopening the wound. And how to teach your nervous system that the threat has passed, even if the memory hasn't disappeared.

For now, simply notice.

Notice when the replay starts. Notice what triggered it. Notice how your body feels during it. And notice how long it takes you to come back to the present moment. These observations are not failures. They are data. And data is how treatment begins.

You are not broken because your mind goes back.
You are not unfaithful because you still remember.
You are not weak because you replay.

You are human. You were hurt. And your system is asking for help, not another rehearsal.

In the Faith Clinic, we don't have silence symptoms. We listen to them long enough to understand what they're asking for. And in the next section, we will begin to explore *why* your brain clings to these loops, *what* they are trying to protect you from, and *how* to start loosening their grip without forcing yourself to "be over it."

Treatment is working; not because the replay is gone, but because you're finally paying attention to it with compassion instead of frustration.

🔲 Faith Prescription

Interrupting The Replay Without Silencing The Truth

The goal of this prescription is *not* to stop your thoughts forcefully. Forced silence creates pressure, and pressure increases rebound. The goal is to interrupt the rehearsal loop long enough for your nervous system to recognize that the threat has passed.

For this stage of treatment, your assignment is not to argue with the replay, correct it, or spiritually override it. Your assignment is to notice the moment the rehearsal begins, and choose not to continue it.

When the replay starts, say internally (or out loud if needed): *"This is the replay. I do not need to finish it."*

Then redirect, not to distraction, but to presence.

This may feel ineffective at first. That's normal. You are retraining a system that has practiced this loop for a long time. Each interruption, even a short one, weakens the pathway. Healing here is measured in shorter loops, not instant silence.

For this phase of treatment:

- Do not demand that the replay stop permanently

- Do not shame yourself when it returns

- Do not confuse awareness with failure

The interruption itself is the healing work.

Prescription Duration: Daily practice
Reassessment: End of Chapter 3

Spiritual Vitamin: Truth That Weakens The Loop

"You will keep in perfect peace those whose minds are steadfast, because they trust in You."
— **Isaiah 26:3**

Notice what this verse does *not* say.

It does not say peace comes from controlling your thoughts.
It does not say peace comes from erasing memory.
It does not say peace comes from getting closure.

Peace comes from ***steadiness***, not suppression.

Steadfastness is not mental perfection, it is gentle redirection back to trust when the mind wanders. Every time you notice the replay and choose to return to the present, you are practicing steadfastness. And peace follows practice, not pressure.

Let this truth nourish you: you are not failing because your mind goes back. You succeed every time you come back.

🕊 Holy Spirit Consult: Awareness Without Judgment

Sit with this question quietly. Do not rush to answer it. Let it surface naturally.

"Holy Spirit, What am I trying to protect myself from when I replay this conversation?"

You may notice themes like:

- Fear of being powerless again

- Fear of being misunderstood

- Fear of not being believed

- Fear of being caught off guard

- Fear of silence meaning agreement

None of these fears are sinful. They are signals. And the Holy Spirit does not remove protection by force, He replaces it with safety.

If nothing comes up immediately, that's okay. Sometimes the consult continues beneath the surface. Trust the process.

🙏 Guided Prayer: Interrupting The Loop Gently

"God, I notice my mind going back again.

I don't want to rehearse this anymore,
but I don't want to ignore it either.

Help me pause without punishing myself.
Help me trust that I don't need to finish
what never got finished safely.

Teach my body that I am not back there.
Teach my mind that I don't need to prepare.
Meet me here, in this moment.

I release the replay, not the truth,
but the need to relive it.

Amen."

✍ Journal Reflection Page: Pattern Awareness

This page is not for storytelling. It is for pattern recognition. Keep your responses simple and honest.

1. The most common time my replay starts is:

____

____

____

____

____

____

2. Right before the replay begins, I usually feel:
☐ Dismissed ☐ Tense ☐ Vulnerable ☐ Overlooked ☐ Unsafe ☐ Unseen

3. The replay usually ends when:
☐ I distract myself
☐ I get emotionally exhausted
☐ Something external interrupts me
☐ I consciously choose to stop

4. One sentence I can use to interrupt the loop is: *"This is the replay. I do not need to finish it."*

5. After I interrupt the replay, my body feels:
☐ Slightly calmer ☐ The same ☐ Resistant ☐ Relieved ☐ Unsure

(All answers are valid. This is data, not grading.)

🛏 Clinic Note: Read Before Moving Forward

Replays do not mean you are stuck.
They mean your system learned to survive.
You are not here to erase memory.
You are here to remove **urgency** from it.
Each interruption teaches your nervous system something new:
that safety does not require rehearsal.

This chapter was not about stopping the loop.
It was about recognizing it without obeying it.

When you are ready, proceed to Chapter 3: *"I Forgave Them" and Other Things You Say to Sound Healed*

We will continue carefully.
We will continue honestly.
And we will continue without rushing your body past its readiness.

Treatment is progressing.

PERSONAL NOTES

Chapter 3

"I Forgave Them" And Other Things You Say To Sound Healed

There are certain phrases that sound like spiritual maturity but function more like emotional camouflage. They roll off their tongue easily. They earn nods in small groups. They shut conversations down quickly. And they protect you from having to explain what still hurts.

"I forgave them" is one of the most convincing.

It's a powerful sentence. It sounds obedient. It sounds like it's finished. It sounds like progress. And most of the time, it's not a lie. You really did forgive them, or at least you intended to. You chose not to retaliate. You released them to God. You stopped engaging outwardly. From the outside, it looks like healing.

But inside, something doesn't feel settled.

This chapter exists because many people are not lying when they say they forgave someone; they're just skipping steps their body never agreed to skip. Forgiveness, when rushed or performed, can become a statement of compliance instead of a process of release. And when that happens, the words may be true, but the system remains unresolved.

In the Faith Clinic, we call this *performative forgiveness,* not because it's fake, but because it's premature.

Performative forgiveness develops when faith communities emphasize speed over safety. When the message is clear: good Christians forgive quickly, quietly, and without needing to talk about it. Over time, people learn to say the right thing before they feel the right thing. They learn how to bypass their own grief to stay spiritually acceptable. They learn how to declare peace while their nervous system stays braced for impact.

And the tragedy is, many of these people genuinely love God. They are not rebellious. They are not holding grudges intentionally. They are doing the best they know how with the tools they were given. The problem is not their heart, it's the framework. Forgiveness becomes something you *announce* instead of something you *experience*.

This is why *"I forgave them"* can coexist with resentment, irritability, emotional shutdown, or sudden reactions that seem disproportionate. The forgiveness may be real at the belief level, but the grief was never processed, the anger was never metabolized, and the boundary confusion was never clarified. So the body keeps holding what the mouth released.

In many cases, saying "I forgave them" becomes a way to end discomfort, both yours and other people's. It signals that the topic is closed. It prevents further questions. It keeps you from being labeled bitter, dramatic, or spiritually immature. It's not manipulation. It's survival.

But survival language eventually stops serving you.

There is also a subtle spiritual pressure tied to forgiveness language that often goes unnamed. People fear that if they admit they're still affected, God will be disappointed. They worry that acknowledging unresolved pain means they're resisting the Holy Spirit. They confuse emotional honesty with spiritual rebellion. So they rush to forgiveness not because they're ready, but because they're afraid of what honesty might imply.

The Faith Clinic challenges that fear directly.

Forgiveness does not require amnesia.
Forgiveness does not require emotional neutrality.
Forgiveness does not require immediate peace.

Forgiveness requires truth, and truth unfolds in stages.

One of the clearest signs of performative forgiveness is the absence of grief. If a significant offense occurred and you moved straight to  forgiveness without mourning what was lost, trust, safety, respect, innocence, belonging, then forgiveness likely became a bypass rather than a bridge. Grief is not optional when something matters. Skipping it doesn't make you strong; it makes the pain resurface later in quieter, more confusing ways.

Another sign is defensiveness when the topic comes up. If mentioning the person or situation makes you tense, irritable, or eager to shut the conversation down with spiritual language, that's not proof you're healed. It's often proof that something still feels exposed. True healing brings flexibility, not rigidity. You don't need to defend forgiveness that has settled properly.

There is also a difference between forgiving someone and accepting what happened without protest. Many people confuse forgiveness with agreement. They think if they admit something hurt deeply, they're somehow accusing God of wrongdoing or questioning His sovereignty. So, they minimize the offense to protect their theology. But forgiveness does not require you to call harm holy. It requires you to stop carrying it alone.

Jesus never rushed people past their pain to prove their faith. He acknowledged wounds before He healed them. He asked questions He already knew the answers to, not to shame, but to bring awareness to what needed care. If the model we follow does not bypass pain, why do we?

This chapter is also where many readers realize that "I forgave them" has sometimes been used as a shield against vulnerability. Saying you forgave them means you don't have to admit how deeply you were affected. It means you don't have to ask for support. It means you don't have to sit with uncomfortable emotions that don't resolve quickly. Forgiveness becomes a way to stay composed rather than a way to get free.

But composure is not the same as peace.

Peace is soft. Peace is spacious. Peace doesn't require constant monitoring of your reactions. Peace doesn't tense up when a name is mentioned. Peace doesn't rehearse explanations in case someone questions your boundaries. Peace doesn't feel brittle.

If your forgiveness feels brittle, it may be unfinished. This does not mean you take it back. It means you deepen it.

The Faith Clinic does not ask you to stop forgiving. It asks you to stop pretending forgiveness is a single moment instead of a layered process. You can forgive someone and still need to grieve. You can forgive someone and still need boundaries. You can forgive someone and still feel anger arise when old patterns repeat. None of that invalidates forgiveness. It simply means your humanity is still participating.

Another common reason performative forgiveness sticks around is unresolved power dynamics. When the offense involved authority, parents, pastors, bosses, mentors, people often forgive quickly because confrontation never felt safe. But what doesn't get named doesn't get neutralized. The system remembers that silence was required, and it keeps the emotional charge alive as a form of self-protection.

That's why some people say they've forgiven, yet feel small, reactive, or hypervigilant in similar situations later. Forgiveness addressed the person, but not the power imbalance. Healing requires both.

This chapter does not ask you to revoke forgiveness or reopen conversations that would cause harm. It is asking you to examine whether your forgiveness was allowed to mature, or whether it was rushed to preserve spiritual image.

And here is the most important truth of this chapter: ***God is not impressed by forgiveness that costs you your honesty.*** He is interested in forgiveness that restores your freedom. If saying "I forgave them" keeps you silent, tense, or emotionally guarded, then forgiveness needs support, not scrutiny.

You are allowed to revise your understanding of what forgiveness looks like. You are allowed to say, "I forgave them, and I'm still healing." You are allowed to admit that forgiveness did not close the wound automatically. You are allowed to return to a process you thought you finished.

That is not regression. That is maturity.

As you move through this chapter, notice where you may have used forgiveness language to protect yourself from discomfort rather than to release pain. Notice where you rushed to spiritual resolution without emotional processing. Notice where you equated healing with silence.

This is not about undoing forgiveness. It's about completing it.

In the Faith Clinic, forgiveness is not a performance you pass. It is a treatment you complete, at your pace, with honesty, and without shame.

And in the next section, we will begin to explore how guilt and obligation often get tangled up in forgiveness language, keeping people stuck in cycles of self-pressure instead of peace.

💊 Faith Prescription

Replacing Performative Forgiveness With Processed Forgiveness

For this stage of treatment, your assignment is not to forgive *again*. It is to stop using forgiveness as a shield.

This prescription asks you to practice truthful language instead of impressive language. For many patients, "I forgave them" has become a reflex, spoken quickly to shut down discomfort, end questions, or protect spiritual image. This week, you are invited to slow that reflex down.

When the urge arises to say, *"I forgave them,"* pause and internally add the rest of the sentence you've been skipping.

"I forgave them, and I'm still healing."
"I forgave them, and it still affected me."
"I forgave them, but I never grieved what was lost."

You do not have to say these sentences out loud to anyone else. This is not about disclosure. This is about internal accuracy.

During this phase of treatment:

- Replace final-sounding statements with honest ones

- Allow forgiveness to coexist with grief

- Stop correcting emotions with theology

Forgiveness matures when it is allowed to breathe.

<u>**Prescription Duration:**</u> 7–10 days
<u>**Reassessment:**</u> After Chapter 4

✒ Spiritual Vitamin: Truth That Removes Pressure

"Blessed are those who mourn, for they shall be comforted."
— **Matthew 5:4**

Notice what this verse does *not* say.

It does not say, *"Blessed are those who move on quickly."*
It does not say, *"Blessed are those who stay composed."*
It does not say, *"Blessed are those who forgive without feeling."*

Comfort follows mourning, not denial.

This means grief is not a detour from healing; it is a doorway to it. If forgiveness skipped mourning, it may need to return—not to reopen the wound, but to allow comfort to finally reach it.

Let this truth nourish you: grief does not compete with forgiveness. It completes it.

🕊 Holy Spirit Consult: Untangling Motive From Obedience

Sit quietly with this question. Do not answer from habit. Let honesty rise before theology.

"Holy Spirit, did I forgive because I was ready, or because I felt pressured to be done?"

You may notice pressure from:

- Church culture

- Family expectations

- Fear of appearing bitter

- Fear of disappointing God

- Discomfort with vulnerability

If pressure surfaces, do not judge yourself. Pressure does not invalidate forgiveness, it simply explains why it stalled.

The Holy Spirit is not interested in rushed obedience. He is interested in restored wholeness.

Guided Prayer: Permission To Be Honest

"God, I meant it when I said I forgave them.
But I also see now where I rushed.
Where I skipped grief.
Where I tried to sound healed instead of be healed.

I don't want forgiveness to be a performance.
I want it to be freedom.

Show me where I used spiritual language
to avoid emotional truth.
Not to shame me—but to release me.

I give You permission to finish
what I started with good intentions.

Amen."

Journal Reflection Page: From Performance To Process

Answer slowly. There is no correct response, only honest ones.

1. When I say, "I forgave them," what emotion do I feel underneath?

☐ Relief ☐ Tension ☐ Sadness ☐ Irritation ☐ Peace ☐ Numbness

2. One thing I never allowed myself to grieve about this situation is:

____

____

____

____

____

____

2. I feel pressure to be "over it" because:

____

____

____

____

____

3. Forgiveness would feel safer if I allowed myself to also say:

____

____

____

____

____

____

5. A truthful sentence I can practice this week is:
"I forgave them, and I am still healing—and that is allowed."

📖 Clinic Note: Read Before Proceeding

Forgiveness that silences you
is not the same as forgiveness that frees you.

You are not undoing forgiveness by revisiting it.
You are deepening it.

This chapter was not about taking words back.
It was about giving them integrity.

In the Faith Clinic, forgiveness is not a finish line.
It is a living process, one that grows more powerful
when honesty is allowed to participate.

When you are ready, proceed to Chapter 4: **Guarding Your Heart or Building a Prison?**

We will continue to untangle protection from peace,
and boundaries from bitterness.

Treatment remains active.
You are doing this correctly.

PERSONAL NOTES

Chapter 4

Guarding Your Heart
Or Building A Prison?

At some point in healing, protection starts to feel like wisdom. You've learned your lesson. You don't overshare anymore. You don't trust quickly. You don't give people the benefit of the doubt the way you used to. You're careful now. Measured. Selective. And if anyone questions it, you already have the verse ready: *"Above all else, guard your heart."*

On the surface, it sounds mature. Responsible, even. But beneath that language, a quieter question lingers, one most people don't want to ask because it threatens the sense of control they worked hard to regain: ***Am I guarding my heart… or am I incarcerating it?***

This chapter exists because protection and imprisonment feel almost identical from the inside. Both reduce risk. Both limit exposure. Both keep pain at bay. The difference is subtle but devastating: one preserves life, the other slowly starves it.

When you've been hurt deeply, especially by people you trusted, your nervous system does exactly what it was designed to do. It adapts. It scans. It tightens boundaries. It reduces vulnerability. These responses are not sinful. 
They are intelligent. They kept you functioning when openness became dangerous. The problem arises when survival strategies outlive the threat and quietly become identity.

What once protected you can eventually isolate you.

Many people mistake emotional shutdown for discernment. They confuse distance with peace. They tell themselves they're calm, but what they really are is contained. Numb enough to function, guarded enough not to be surprised, detached enough not to be disappointed. It looks like maturity. It feels like control. But control is not the same as safety, and it is certainly not the same as healing.

This is where "guard your heart" gets misused.

That verse was never meant to authorize emotional lockdown. Guarding your heart means protecting what flows *into* it, not barricading what flows *out* of it. It was written to promote wisdom, not withdrawal. Discernment, not disappearance. Yet many people, after being wounded, reinterpret guarding as sealing. They don't just filter access; they eliminate it.

And the heart, unlike a fortress, does not thrive under lockdown.

One of the clearest indicators that guarding has crossed into imprisonment is **rigidity**. When your boundaries leave no room for nuance. When curiosity feels unsafe. When connection feels suspicious by default. When your first instinct is not discernment but distance. True wisdom is flexible. It adjusts based on context, not fear. Prisons, on the other hand, operate on absolutes.

Another indicator is *constant* monitoring. If you find yourself always scanning, reading tone, watching for shifts, bracing for disappointment; that's not peace. That's hypervigilance. And hypervigilance is exhausting because it requires your system to always stay alert. It convinces you that rest equals risk.

This is why so many people say, "I'm fine being alone," while simultaneously feeling lonely. They're not lying. Solitude feels safer than connection when connection once cost too much. But safety built on isolation is fragile. It protects you from pain, yes, but it also blocks intimacy, joy, and repair.

In the Faith Clinic, we name this clearly: boundaries that are rooted in fear will always feel like confinement. Boundaries rooted in wisdom feel spacious. They don't suffocate you. They don't require constant explanation. They don't need to be defended aggressively. They simply exist, and they protect themselves without punishing.

So how do you tell the difference?

Ask yourself this: *Does my guardedness increase my capacity for life, or decrease it?* Do you feel more available to peace, or more preoccupied with control? Do your boundaries help you show up honestly, or do they keep you from showing up at all?

Many people cling to guardedness because it gives them a sense of agency after a season of powerlessness. That makes sense. When you couldn't control what happened to you, control became synonymous with safety. But control is a poor substitute for healing. It manages fear; it doesn't resolve it.

This is where unforgiveness quietly feeds the prison. When the offense hasn't been fully processed, guarding your heart becomes a way to avoid reopening unresolved pain. You tell yourself you're wise, but what you're really doing is protecting a wound that never closed. And because the wound is still tender, anything that resembles closeness feels like a threat.

So, you guard harder.
You narrow access further.
You reinforce the walls.

Over time, the prison becomes familiar. Predictable. And familiarity starts to feel like peace, even when it isn't.

Another sign you've crossed the line is **identity fusion**. You no longer see guarding as something you do; it's something you *are*. "I'm just guarded." "I don't trust people." "I keep to myself." These statements feel neutral, but they're confessions of resignation. They suggest that the prison has become home.

Healing doesn't require you to abandon boundaries. It requires you to re-examine the motive behind them.

Are your boundaries helping you engage life more honestly, or helping you avoid it more efficiently?

There's also a spiritual layer to this that deserves attention. Many people believe God prefers them guarded. That He's pleased when they're cautious, reserved, emotionally restrained. They fear that openness equals naïveté, that vulnerability equals disobedience. But Scripture paints a very different picture. God does not invite His people into cages. He invites them into freedom, with wisdom.

Freedom is not reckless. But it is alive.

Jesus did not operate from guardedness. He operated from discernment. He withdrew, when necessary, but He also engaged deeply. He didn't give everyone access, but He didn't shut everyone out. And when He was wounded, He didn't build prisons, He healed, forgave, and kept moving toward love.

This is not a call to overexpose yourself or reopen unsafe relationships. This is a call to stop equating emotional shutdown with spiritual maturity.

If guarding your heart has made you smaller, quieter, more distant, or more rigid, it's worth asking whether what you're calling wisdom is fear wearing theology.

The Faith Clinic does not ask you to tear down your walls overnight. Walls exist for a reason. But it does ask you to unlock the door. To remember that boundaries are meant to regulate access, not eliminate it. To allow yourself to be open *selectively* rather than closed universally.

One of the most compassionate things you can do is acknowledge that your guardedness once helped you survive. Thank it. And then ask if it's still serving you.

Because survival mode is not meant to be permanent residence.

As you sit with this chapter, you may notice discomfort. Guardedness feels safe because it's familiar. Questioning it can feel like inviting risk back into your life. But healing is not about removing protection, it's about upgrading it. Moving from reflexive defense to intentional discernment. From fear-based walls to wisdom-based boundaries.

You are allowed to be protected *and* open.
You are allowed to be wise *and* warm.
You are allowed to guard your heart without imprisoning it.

In the Faith Clinic, we believe that peace is not found behind bars, no matter how carefully they were built. Peace is found when safety is restored internally, not enforced externally.

In the next section, we will begin to explore how guilt and obligation often keep people locked inside boundaries God never asked them to maintain, and how to step out without fear.

⊘ Faith Prescription

From Fear-Based Guarding To Wisdom-Based Boundaries

For this phase of treatment, your assignment is not to open yourself up indiscriminately. It is to examine the motive behind your guardedness. Guarding your heart is not the problem. Guarding it without discernment is.

This prescription invites you to pause before reinforcing walls and ask one clarifying question: *"Is this boundary protecting my healing, or protecting my fear?"*

You are not asked to lower boundaries that keep you safe. You are asked to stop maintaining boundaries that keep you isolated. This distinction matters.

During this stage of treatment:

- Do not dismantle boundaries impulsively

- Do not justify emotional shutdown with scripture

- Do not confuse calmness with peace

Instead, practice selective openness. This means allowing yourself to notice where connection feels possible without forcing it. Wisdom does not rush. But it also does not imprison.

For the next week, when you feel the urge to pull away, do not act immediately. Pause. Breathe. Ask what you are protecting, and whether that protection still fits the present moment.

Prescription Duration: 7–10 days
Reassessment: After Chapter 5

Spiritual Vitamin: Truth That Creates Space

"Where the Spirit of the Lord is, there is freedom."
— 2 Corinthians 3:17

Freedom is not recklessness.
Freedom is not overexposure.
Freedom is not lack of boundaries.

Freedom is ***movement***.

If your guardedness has eliminated movement, movement toward trust, connection, curiosity, or joy, it may be time to let the Spirit redefine safety. God does not heal by shrinking your life. He heals by restoring your capacity to engage it wisely.

Let this truth nourish you: boundaries shaped by the Spirit feel spacious, not suffocating.

🕊 Holy Spirit Consult: Discernment Over Defense

Sit quietly and reflect on this question. Do not answer quickly. Let honesty surface first.

"Holy Spirit, which of my boundaries were built for survival, and which ones are You inviting me to update?"

You may notice:

- Boundaries formed in seasons of chaos that no longer exist

- Walls built to protect a wound that has already begun healing

- Patterns of withdrawal that once kept you safe but now keep you distant

The Holy Spirit does not remove protection before replacing it with wisdom. Trust that any invitation to update boundaries will come with clarity, not pressure.

🙏 Guided Prayer:
Releasing The Prison Without Losing Protection

God, I learned how to guard myself because I had to.
I learned how to stay contained because openness once hurt.

I don't want to live behind walls You never asked me to build.
But I also don't want to be reckless with my heart.

Teach me the difference between wisdom and fear.
Show me where protection became isolation.
Help me trust You to keep me safe without making me small.

I release the need to stay locked down.
I receive the ability to discern wisely.

Amen.

Journal Reflection Page: Boundaries With Honesty

Answer gently. This is not a test. This is awareness.

1. One boundary I currently hold that feels heavy or rigid is:

____

____

____

____

____

2. I originally built this boundary because:

____

____

____

____

____

3. This boundary now affects my life by:
☐ Increasing peace
☐ Preventing connection
☐ Creating emotional distance
☐ Making me feel safe but lonely

4. A boundary that feels healthy and spacious is:

____

____

____

____

____

5. One sentence I can practice this week is:
"I am allowed to be protected without being imprisoned."

💾 Clinic Note: Read Before Proceeding

You are not wrong for building walls.
You are wise to question whether you still need them.

Boundaries rooted in fear shrink your life.
Boundaries rooted in wisdom support it.

This chapter was not about tearing anything down.
It was about unlocking what no longer needs to stay sealed.

In the Faith Clinic, we do not confuse distance with discernment
or isolation with maturity.

When you are ready, proceed to Chapter 5: ***When Your Body Knows You're Not Over It***

We will continue gently,
working with your nervous system instead of against it.

Treatment remains active.
You are healing with integrity.

CHAPTER NOTES

____

____

____

____

____

____

____

____

____

____

____

____

____

PERSONAL NOTES

Chapter 5

When Your Body Knows You're Not Over It

Your body is honest in ways your language has learned to soften.

You can say you're fine while your shoulders stay tight. You can say you've forgiven while your stomach knots up. You can say you've moved on while your chest reacts before your mind has time to explain.

This chapter exists because long before you consciously admit you're not over something, *your body already knows*.

One of the most frustrating experiences in healing is realizing that your beliefs have changed, your intentions are sincere, and your faith feels solid, yet your physical reactions haven't caught up. You walk into a room and feel uneasy without knowing why. You hear a name and feel heat rise in your chest. You encounter a situation that reminds you of the offense and your heart rate spikes before you can pray about it. And you wonder, *Why is my body betraying me?*

It's not betraying you.
It's communicating.

The body does not operate on spiritual declarations. It operates on learned safety. And when an offense involved shock, abandonment, humiliation, or powerlessness, your body adapted to survive it. That adaptation does not disappear just because you've forgiven. It disappears when your nervous system learns, through repetition, that the danger has passed. This is why forgiveness can feel complete in your spirit but unfinished in your physiology.

In the Faith Clinic, we treat this not as disobedience, but as incomplete regulation.

Your nervous system has one primary job: keep you alive. It does not prioritize politeness, theology, or appearances. It prioritizes pattern recognition. When something in the present resembles something that once hurt you, your body responds automatically. Not because it wants to relive the pain, but because it wants to prevent it from happening again.

That response often shows up as tension, shallow breathing, irritability, fatigue, or emotional shutdown. These are not random reactions. They are protective reflexes.

The problem is that most people interpret these reflexes as proof they're failing at forgiveness.

So they push harder spiritually.
They pray louder.
They quote more scripture.
They scold themselves for "still reacting."

And in doing so, they create more internal conflict.

Your body doesn't calm down when it's criticized. It calms down when it feels safe.

That's a truth we rarely talk about in faith spaces. We expect obedience to override biology. But God designed the body. He understands how it works. And He does not heal by shaming systems He created for survival.

When Jesus encountered people with physical responses, trembling, falling, withdrawing, He did not demand composure before offering care. He met them where their bodies already were.

Why do we expect ourselves to be different?

Many people who struggle with unforgiveness are not emotionally stuck; they are somatically unresolved. The event ended, but the body never completed the stress response. There was no safety afterward. No validation. No regulation. So the body stayed on alert.

That alertness becomes your baseline.

You may notice it as:

- Difficulty relaxing fully

- Trouble sleeping

- Being easily startled

- Feeling drained after social interaction

- A constant sense of "being on edge"

And because these sensations don't feel spiritual, they're often ignored or minimized. People assume they need more faith, more prayer, more discipline. Rarely do they consider that they may need more gentleness.

This chapter invites you to stop fighting your body and start listening to it. When your body reacts, it is not saying, *"You haven't forgiven."* It is saying, *"I don't feel safe yet."*

Those are very different messages.

One leads to shame.
The other leads to healing.

Another reason the body holds on is because many offenses never came with repair. There was no apology. No accountability. No acknowledgment. No moment where safety was restored relationally. In those cases, the body learned that harm can happen without warning, and it stays vigilant accordingly.

Forgiveness does not magically resolve that lesson.

This is especially true when the offense came from someone you depended on emotionally or spiritually. The closer the attachment, the deeper the imprint. When trust is violated, the body learns to protect itself preemptively. That protection can look like withdrawal, emotional numbing, or hyper-awareness.

None of those mean you are unhealed.
They mean you adapted.

And adaptations require updates, not judgment.

Another layer to this is grief. When grief is bypassed, it often lodges in the body. Uncried tears show up as tight throats. Unspoken anger shows up as clenched jaws. Unacknowledged fear shows up as shallow breathing. The body becomes the storage unit for emotions you were never allowed to feel fully.

Forgiveness without grief leaves the body holding the residue.

That's why some people feel worse after trying to "move on." Their spirit released, but their body never got permission to finish what it started.

In the Faith Clinic, we normalize this. We do not rush regulation. We do not force calm. We do not demand peace as proof of progress. We look for shorter recovery times, not immediate neutrality.

Healing in the body looks like:

- Noticing tension sooner

- Calming down faster

- Recovering more gently

- Feeling safer more often

It does not look like never reacting again.

If you're reading this and realizing your body has been trying to tell you something for a long time, that is not discouraging news. It's hopeful. Because what can be listened to can be healed.

Your body is not your enemy.
It is your witness.

It remembers what you survived.
It remembers what you didn't get.
And it remembers what it took to keep you
functioning.

This chapter is not asking you to relive pain or dissect every sensation. It's asking you to stop interpreting physical reactions as spiritual failure. It's asking you to partner with your body instead of overriding it.

As you move forward, pay attention to when your body tightens, not to judge it, but to reassure it. Let those moments become signals to slow down, ground yourself, and return to the present. You don't need to force your body to forgive. You need to help it feel safe enough to let go.

And in the next section, we will begin to explore how to work *with* your nervous system instead of against it, so healing becomes embodied, not just believed.

☮ Faith Prescription

Regulating the Body Before Requiring Release

For this stage of treatment, your assignment is not to make your body behave. It is to befriend it. Your body does not need correction, it needs reassurance.

This prescription asks you to stop interpreting physical reactions as spiritual resistance. Tight shoulders, shallow breathing, sudden fatigue, irritability, or emotional shutdown are not signs of failure. They are signals that your nervous system is still protecting you.

When your body reacts, do not scold it. Do not rush to override it with scripture. Do not demand calm. Instead, respond with curiosity.

Silently say:
"Thank you for trying to protect me. I am safe right now."

This is not indulgence. It is regulation.

During this phase of treatment:

- Do not force yourself to relax

- Do not demand peace on command

- Do not spiritualize physical reactions away

Instead, practice gentle grounding. Notice where your body feels tense. Slow your breathing. Drop your shoulders. Place your feet on the floor. Look around and remind yourself where you are.

Safety must be felt, not declared.

Prescription Duration: Daily practice
Reassessment: After Chapter 6

Spiritual Vitamin: Truth That Calms The Body

"Peace I leave with you; My peace I give you.
I do not give to you as the world gives.
Do not let your hearts be troubled."
— John 14:27

Jesus offers peace as a *gift*, not a demand.

This peace is not adrenaline-free composure. It is not emotional suppression. It is not pretending nothing affects you. It is a presence that settles slowly and stays longer with practice.

Let this truth nourish you: peace is learned through repetition, not forced through discipline. Your body will catch up as safety is practiced consistently.

🕊 Holy Spirit Consult: Listening To The Body With God

Sit quietly and place one hand on your chest or stomach. Breathe slowly. Then ask:

Holy Spirit, what is my body trying to protect me from right now?

You may notice:

- Fear of being caught off guard
- Fear of emotional overwhelm
- Fear of vulnerability
- Fear of repeating an old pattern

Do not argue with what comes up. Let it be named. The Holy Spirit does not rush protection away, He replaces it with trust.

If nothing surfaces, that's okay. Sometimes regulation comes before revelation.

🙏 Guided Prayer: Teaching The Body Safety

"God, My body reacts before I can explain.
I don't want to fight it anymore.

Thank You for designing me with the ability to survive.
Thank You that my reactions are not rebellion.

Help my body learn what my spirit already believes.
Help me notice tension without judging it.
Help me feel safe in the present moment.

I receive Your peace, not as pressure,
but as presence.

Amen."

📝 Journal Reflection Page: Body Awareness Without Shame

Keep responses simple. This is not analysis. This is awareness.

1. When my body reacts, I usually feel:
☐ Tight ☐ Tired ☐ Alert ☐ Numb ☐ Restless ☐ Overwhelmed

2. The situation that most often triggers a body response is:

____

____

____

____

____

____

3. One place in my body that holds tension is:

____

4. When I slow down and ground myself, my body responds by:
☐ Calming slightly ☐ Resisting ☐ Feeling safer ☐ Feeling uncertain

5. One sentence I can use to reassure myself is:
"I am safe right now. My body does not need to stay on guard."

📖 Clinic Note: Read Before Moving Forward

Your body is not holding a grudge.
It is holding a memory.

Healing does not begin when the body stops reacting.
It begins when the body stops being punished for reacting.

This chapter was not about controlling your nervous system.
It was about earning its trust.

As safety increases, reactions will shorten.
As trust deepens, peace will last longer.

When you are ready, proceed to Chapter 6: ***Jesus Didn't Minimize Pain, He Healed It***

We will continue to integrate faith with compassion,
truth with tenderness,
and healing with wisdom.

Treatment remains active.
You are healing on every level.

Chapter 6

Jesus Didn't Minimize Pain, He Healed It

If Jesus were walking through most modern faith spaces today, He would probably make people uncomfortable, not because He challenged belief, but because He refused to rush past pain. He would not reward composure over honesty. He would not confuse silence with maturity. And He certainly would not tell wounded people to "just forgive" without first acknowledging what hurt.

This chapter exists because many people have learned a version of faith that unintentionally minimizes pain in the name of obedience. A version that praises quick forgiveness, quiet suffering, and emotional restraint as spiritual virtues, while overlooking the fact that Jesus consistently did the opposite. He didn't dismiss pain. He didn't spiritualize it away. He didn't treat wounds like inconveniences to be managed. He healed them.

Minimization is subtle. It rarely sounds cruel. It sounds spiritual.

"It wasn't that bad."
"God used it for good."
"At least it made you stronger."
"Other people have it worse."
"Forgive and move on."

None of these statements are entirely false. But when they are used too early, they don't heal, they silence. They teach people to override their own experience to stay acceptable. And when pain is minimized, it doesn't disappear. It relocates. It moves into the body. It embeds itself in patterns. It resurfaces later as anxiety, numbness, resentment, or chronic self-protection.

Jesus never healed people by telling them to downplay their suffering.

When blind men cried out, He didn't tell them to lower their voice and be grateful for what they *did* have. He asked, "What do you want Me to do for you?" When a woman who had been bleeding for twelve years reached out in desperation, He didn't rebuke her for being dramatic. He stopped. He turned toward her. He called her *daughter*. When Lazarus died, Jesus didn't quote theology to Martha and Mary to speed them past grief. He wept.

Let that sit for a moment.

Jesus wept, even though He knew resurrection was coming.

That alone dismantles the idea that faith requires emotional bypassing. If knowing the outcome did not exempt Jesus from grieving the pain, why do we think it should exempt us?

One of the most damaging messages many believers internalize is that acknowledging pain somehow dishonors God. That if you admit something hurt deeply, you're questioning His sovereignty or lacking trust. But Jesus never treated pain as a threat to faith. He treated it as a place where faith could meet compassion.

Minimization often enters when people confuse endurance with healing. Yes, endurance is biblical. Yes, perseverance matters. But endurance without care leads to hardness, not wholeness. Jesus didn't just endure the brokenness of the world, He confronted it, touched it, and restored what it damaged.

In the Faith Clinic, we name this clearly: anything that requires you to silence your pain to stay faithful is not healing, it's suppression.

Suppressed pain does not sanctify you. It exhausts you.

Another reason pain gets minimized is because people fear it will consume them. They worry that if they acknowledge how bad it really was, they'll fall apart. So they keep it contained.

Manageable. Theologically neat. But Jesus didn't heal by keeping wounds small. He healed by touching them directly.

Think about the man with the withered hand. Jesus didn't say, "At least you still have another hand." He didn't tell him to be grateful and adapt. He told him to stretch out the hand, the very place of limitation, exposure, and vulnerability. Healing required acknowledgment.

Minimization is often learned early, especially in environments where emotional expression wasn't safe. Many people were taught, explicitly or implicitly, that strong faith looks calm, controlled, and unbothered. So, they learned to swallow reactions. To stay composed. To spiritualize discomfort. Over time, they became excellent at functioning while wounded.

But functioning is not the same as healing.

Jesus didn't just want people to function. He wanted them restored.

This chapter is especially important for those who feel guilty for still being affected. If you've ever thought, *"I shouldn't still feel this way,"* or *"I'm past this spiritually, why is it still showing up?* "that guilt did not come from Jesus. He never shamed people for lingering pain. He addressed it.

There's also a critical distinction between forgiveness and minimization that often gets blurred. Forgiveness releases the offense. Minimization denies its impact. Forgiveness says, *"I'm no longer holding this against you."* Minimization says, *"It didn't really matter."* Those are not the same and confusing them often delays healing.

Jesus forgave without minimizing. On the cross, He said, "Father, forgive them," not "This doesn't hurt." He acknowledged the pain fully while releasing the offense. That's the model we're invited into—not numbness, not denial, but honesty paired with grace.

Another place minimization shows up is when people rush to meaning too quickly. "Everything happens for a reason" may be true in the long arc of redemption, but it can be deeply harmful when used to bypass grief. Jesus did not explain suffering away. He entered it. He sat with it. He healed in relationship, not rhetoric.

If your pain was real, it deserves real attention.

Healing in the Faith Clinic does not begin with asking, *"What lesson did I learn?"* It begins with asking, *"What did this cost me?"* Because until the cost is acknowledged, the body continues to hold the debt.

This chapter invites you to release the pressure to be unfazed. To stop apologizing for pain that was legitimate. To recognize that Jesus does not measure faith by how little you feel, but by how honestly you bring what you feel into His presence.

You do not honor God by minimizing your wounds. You honor Him by letting Him tend to them.

Jesus never asked people to prove they were healed before He healed them. He met them in their need, not their composure. And the same invitation stands for you.

As you continue forward, you may notice emotions surfacing that you once dismissed as unnecessary or excessive. That's not regression. That's access. Healing often feels like vulnerability before it feels like relief.

In the next section, we will explore how Jesus 'approach to pain gives us permission to slow down forgiveness, integrate compassion, and allow healing to be embodied, not just believed.

Faith Prescription

Permission Before Progress

For this phase of treatment, your assignment is not to explain your pain. It is to stop minimizing it.

Minimization delays healing because it tells your system that honesty is unsafe. When you downplay what hurt you, whether to stay spiritual, avoid discomfort, or protect others, you teach your body that pain must be managed quietly instead of healed fully.

This prescription invites you to practice ***permission***.

Permission to say:

- *"That really hurt."*

- *"I'm still affected."*

- *"I don't need to justify this."*

You are not asked to relive the pain. You are asked to acknowledge its impact without correcting yourself.

During this phase of treatment:

- Do not rush to meaning

- Do not soften the story to make it easier to hold

- Do not spiritualize pain away

Instead, allow pain to be named plainly, without apology.

Jesus did not heal what people minimized.
He healed what they brought to Him honestly.

<u>**Prescription Duration**</u>: As needed
<u>**Reassessment**</u>: After Chapter 7

🧬 Spiritual Vitamin: Truth That Validates Pain

"Jesus wept."
— **John 11:35**

This verse is short, but it is profound.

Jesus knew resurrection was coming, and He still wept.

That means tears are not a lack of faith.
Grief is not spiritual weakness.
Acknowledging pain does not delay redemption.

Let this truth nourish you: if Jesus did not minimize suffering, neither should you. Healing flows where honesty is allowed.

🕊 Holy Spirit Consult:
Inviting Compassion Where Minimization Lived

Sit quietly and ask this without rushing to answer:

"Holy Spirit, where have I been minimizing my pain to stay acceptable?"

You may notice:

- Pain you downplayed to avoid conflict

- Hurt you softened to protect someone else's image

- Experiences you dismissed because others had it worse

- Grief you never allowed yourself to feel fully

Whatever surfaces is not something to judge. It is something to bring into the light gently. The Holy Spirit does not shame pain, He heals it.

🙏 Guided Prayer: Releasing The Need To Downplay

"Jesus, You never rushed people past their pain.
You never asked them to pretend it didn't hurt.

I release the need to be unfazed.
I let go of the pressure to explain away my wounds.

I bring You what actually happened—
not cleaned up,
not minimized,
not justified.

Meet me where I am,
not where I think I should be.

Amen."

📝 Journal Reflection Page: Naming Without Minimizing

Respond honestly. This is not a theology exercise. It is a healing one.

1. One experience I've minimized that still affects me is:

____

____

____

____

____

2. I downplayed this pain because:
☐ I didn't want to seem weak
☐ I was told to move on
☐ Others expected me to forgive quickly
☐ I didn't feel safe naming it
☐ I thought faith required silence

3. What this experience cost me was:

____

____

____

____

4. If Jesus were sitting with me in this moment, I imagine He would say:

____

____

____

____

5. One sentence I can practice this week is:
"My pain mattered, and God is not threatened by my honesty."

📖 Clinic Note: Read Before Proceeding

Minimizing pain does not make you holy. It makes you tired.

Jesus did not heal people by rushing them. He healed them by staying with them.

This chapter was not about reopening wounds.
It was about removing the pressure to pretend they never existed.

In the Faith Clinic, we believe healing begins where permission replaces performance.

When you are ready, proceed to Chapter 7: ***The Offense Ended, But the Attachment Didn't***

We will continue to gently untangle memory from meaning,
pain from identity,
and survival from safety.

Treatment is deepening.
You are healing the way Jesus heals, honestly, compassionately, and completely.

Chapter 7

The Offense Ended, But The Attachment Didn't

One of the most confusing parts of healing is realizing that the event is over, but your internal connection to it is not. The relationship may have ended. The conversation may never happen. The chapter of your life may be closed externally. And yet, internally, something still feels tethered. You don't want to go back. You don't even want contact. But part of you still checks in, still reacts, still carries the weight of what happened as if it's ongoing.

This chapter exists because closure is not the same as detachment.

Many people believe that once an offense ends, attachment should end automatically. That if time has passed, distance has been created, or forgiveness has been spoken, the emotional connection should dissolve on its own. When it doesn't, they assume something is wrong with them. They wonder why they still care. Why they still feel affected. Why a situation that is technically "over" still has access to their inner world.

The truth is, attachment does not follow timelines. It follows *impact*.

Attachment forms when something mattered, when there was hope, trust, expectation, dependency, or identity involved. And when an offense disrupts those bonds without repair, the attachment doesn't disappear. It lingers. Not because you want it to, but because your system is still trying to make sense of what happened.

This is why you can intellectually accept that the offense is over while emotionally feeling like it's unresolved. The mind moves forward faster than the heart. And the heart moves forward faster than the body. Healing has layers, and attachment lives in all three.

Unresolved attachment often gets misinterpreted as unforgiveness. But they are not the same. Forgiveness releases the offense. Attachment holds onto the meaning.

You may have forgiven what they did, but you're still attached to:

- The version of yourself you were before it happened

- The relationship you thought you had

- The future you imagined

- The validation you never received

- The apology that never came

Those attachments don't dissolve just because the event ended. They dissolve when they are grieved, reoriented, and replaced with something truer.

This is where many people get stuck. They assume that letting go of attachment means excusing the harm or minimizing the loss. So they cling to it quietly, believing it's the only way to honor what happened. But attachment is not honoring pain, it's extending its influence.

Another reason attachment lingers is because it provides a sense of control. If you stay emotionally connected to the offense, you don't have to fully face the uncertainty that comes with release. Attachment keeps the story alive, and stories, especially painful ones, can feel safer than blank space. Letting go means stepping into a version of life where that chapter no longer defines you, and that can feel disorienting.

For some, attachment becomes identity.

You don't just remember the offense, you organize your worldview around it. You become the one who was betrayed, overlooked, abandoned, or misunderstood. That identity shapes your expectations, your boundaries, and your self-talk. It explains why you are the way you are now. And while it may not feel good, it feels *known*.

Healing threatens that identity.

Letting go of attachment doesn't just release pain; it releases the role you've been living in. And roles, even painful ones, can be hard to relinquish when they've given your story coherence.

There's also a biological component here that often goes unnoticed. Attachment activates the same neural pathways as bonding. When a bond is broken abruptly or traumatically, the nervous system doesn't immediately recalibrate. It stays alert, connected, scanning for resolution. That's why you may still feel pulled toward the memory, still feel emotional spikes when reminded, still feel unfinished—even if you logically know it's done.

This is not weakness. It's physiology.

Another layer of attachment comes from unfinished emotional expression. If you never got to say what you needed to say, feel what you needed to feel, or receive what you needed to receive, the attachment persists as an open loop. The system keeps holding onto the connection because it's still waiting for completion.

That completion does not always come from the other person.

This is one of the hardest truths in healing: some attachments remain not because reconciliation is needed, but because internal completion is. The nervous system wants acknowledgment, not access. Closure, not contact. Validation, not vindication.

And here's where faith often gets misapplied. People are told to "let it go" without being taught how to detach without dissociating. Detachment doesn't mean pretending it didn't matter. It means reclaiming your emotional energy from a place that no longer deserves to hold it.

Detachment is not coldness.
It is clarity.

You can detach and still care about what happened.
You can detach and still grieve.
You can detach and still acknowledge the impact.

Detachment simply means the offense no longer gets to organize your inner life.

One of the reasons detachment feels so threatening is because attachment has been serving a purpose. It may have been protecting you from repeating the same mistake. It may have been keeping you alert. It may have been reminding you to stay guarded. Letting go can feel like abandoning those protections. But true detachment doesn't remove wisdom, it removes hypervigilance.

Another reason attachment lingers is unfinished forgiveness toward yourself. You may still be attached to the offense because you're still judging yourself for what you didn't see, didn't say, or didn't prevent. As long as self-blame remains active, the attachment stays reinforced. The story keeps replaying to fix what can't be fixed.

Detachment requires compassion, especially toward yourself.

Jesus understood attachment. He didn't shame people for clinging to what hurt them. He invited them to something new. When He healed people, He often said, "Go," not just "Be healed." Healing was paired with movement. Reorientation. A turning away from what once defined them toward what now could.

This chapter is not asking you to force detachment. Forced detachment is dissociation. It looks like numbness, indifference, or emotional shutdown. That is not freedom. That is avoidance with better boundaries.

Healthy detachment is gradual. It happens as grief is honored, safety is restored, and identity expands beyond the wound. It happens when the attachment no longer feels necessary for protection or meaning.

As you reflect on this chapter, notice where attachment may still be present, not with judgment, but with curiosity. Ask yourself:

- What am I still holding onto here?

- What did this situation give me that I'm afraid to lose if I let go?

- What part of me is still waiting for something that may never come?

These questions are not meant to trap you. They are meant to orient you.

The offense ended. That part is true.
But attachment doesn't end on command.
It ends when the system no longer needs it.

Healing in the Faith Clinic is not about ripping attachments away. It's about outgrowing them.

And as we move forward, we will begin to explore how to release attachment without losing wisdom, how to grieve what never came, and how to step into a present that is no longer organized around a past injury.

You are not behind because attachment remains. You are human. And you are closer to freedom than you think.

Releasing Attachment Without Losing Wisdom

For this phase of treatment, your assignment is not to force detachment. Forced detachment creates numbness, not freedom. Your assignment is to identify what the attachment has been doing for you and gently release its job.

Attachment remains because it once served a purpose. It may have protected you from repeating harm. It may have preserved meaning when things ended abruptly. It may have kept you alert, prepared, or emotionally guarded. Thank the attachment for what it did, then let it retire.

This week, I will practice internal completion.

When you notice the pull toward the offense, say: *"This no longer needs my energy to keep me safe."*

Then redirect your attention, not away from truth, but toward the present.

During this stage of treatment:

- Do not shame yourself for lingering attachment

- Do not confuse detachment with indifference

- Do not rush grief out of the process

Detachment is not disappearance.
Detachment is reassignment of emotional energy.

Prescription Duration: 7–10 days
Reassessment: After Chapter 8

✤ Spiritual Vitamin: Truth That Breaks The Tether

"Forget the former things; do not dwell on the past.

See, I am doing a new thing."
— Isaiah 43:18–19

"Forget" here does not mean erase.
It means **stop living there**.

God does not ask you to deny what shaped you.
He invites you to stop organizing your present around it.

Let this truth nourish you: the new thing God is doing does not require you to stay attached to the old pain to remain wise.

✤ Holy Spirit Consult: Identifying the Hidden Tie

Sit quietly and ask this with honesty and gentleness: *"Holy Spirit, what am I still attached to in this story, and why?"*

You may notice:

- A hope that never materializes.

- A version of yourself you miss.

- Validation you never received.

- An apology that never came.

- A sense of control attachment provides.

Whatever surfaces is not something to correct. It is something to acknowledge so it can be released without fear. The Holy Spirit replaces attachment with assurance, not emptiness.

🙏 Guided Prayer: Completing What Never Closed

"God, I see now that I'm still holding on, not to the person,

but to what the situation meant to me.

I release the need for resolution that may never come.
I release the version of myself that existed before the hurt.
I release the hope that kept me tethered.

I don't let go to forget.
I let go to live.

Help me detach without hardening.
Help me grieve without getting stuck.
Help me move forward without losing wisdom.

Amen."

📝 Journal Reflection Page: Untangling Attachment

Answer gently. This is not about fixing, it's about clarity.

1. One thing I am still emotionally attached to in this situation is:

____

____

____

____

____

____

____

____

2. This attachment has been protecting me from:

____

____

____

____

3. If I fully released this attachment, I'm afraid I would lose:

____

____

____

____

4. Something new God may be inviting me into is:

____

____

____

____

5. A sentence I can practice this week is:
   "I release what no longer needs to hold my attention."

🏥 Clinic Note: Read Before Proceeding

Attachment is not disobedience.
It is unfinished processing.

You are not weak for feeling tethered.
You are brave for loosening the tie.

This chapter was not about cutting bonds violently.
It was about allowing them to dissolve naturally
as safety, grief, and truth are honored.

In the Faith Clinic, detachment is not loss.
It is recovery of self.

When you are ready, proceed to Chapter 8: ***Forgiveness Isn't an Event: It's a Nervous System Reset***

We will continue integrating faith with physiology,
truth with tenderness,
and release with regulation.

Treatment is advancing.
You are reclaiming your emotional freedom: one layer at a time.

What is one small step of faithful presence I can practice this week?

PERSONAL NOTES

Chapter 8

Forgiveness Isn't An Event: It's A Nervous System Reset

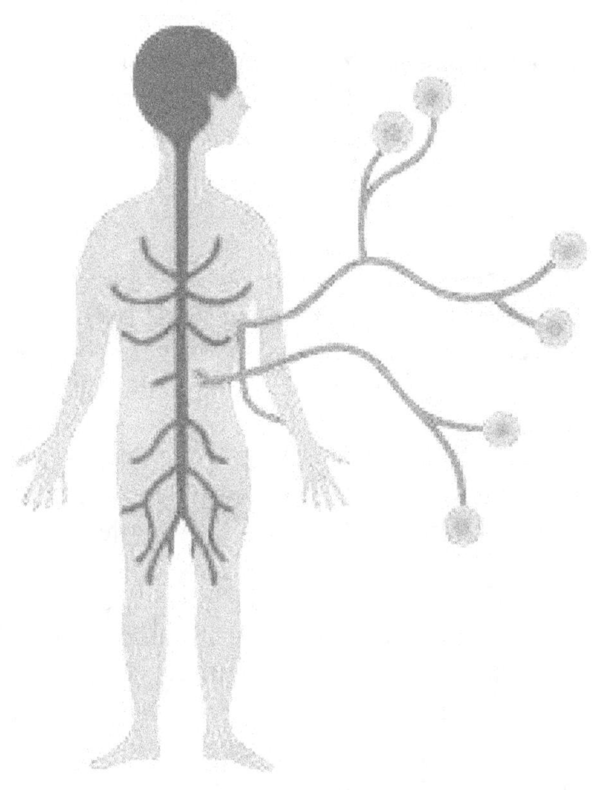

Most people treat forgiveness like a moment. A decision. A prayer you say once and then move on from. You forgive, you close the chapter, and you expect your internal world to fall into alignment immediately. And when it doesn't, when your body still reacts, your thoughts still loop, your emotions still spike, you assume something went wrong. Either you didn't forgive "correctly," or forgiveness itself doesn't work the way you were promised.

This chapter exists to tell you the truth no one explained: ***forgiveness is not a moment; it's a physiological recalibration***.

You can decide to forgive in a second. Your nervous system cannot.

Forgiveness, when it's real and lasting, is not just a spiritual choice. It's a retraining of your body's threat response. It's teaching your system that the danger has passed, that it no longer needs to stay braced, alert, or reactive. And that kind of learning happens through repetition, not declarations.

This is why so many sincere, faith-filled people feel confused and discouraged. They forgave with their will, but their body never caught up. Their spirit moved on, but their nervous system stayed on guard. And instead of understanding this gap, they blamed themselves for it.

In the Faith Clinic, we name this clearly: forgiveness that doesn't reach the nervous system will always feel fragile.

Your nervous system is designed to learn through experience. It doesn't respond to intentions alone. It responds to patterns. Safety patterns. Consistency patterns. Repetition patterns. If an offense shocked your system, especially if it involved betrayal, abandonment, humiliation, or powerlessness, your body learned something in that moment: *stay alert, don't relax, don't trust easily.*

Forgiveness doesn't erase that lesson. It replaces it. And replacement takes time.

Think about how the body learns anything. You don't lift a weight once and expect strength to appear. You don't sleep well one night and expect chronic exhaustion to disappear. You don't calm yourself down once and expect lifelong regulation. The nervous system learns through practice.

This is why forgiveness often feels like it's working one day and not the next. One moment you feel peaceful. The next, you're triggered again. That doesn't mean forgiveness fails. It means your system is in training.

The problem is, most people don't know they're training their nervous system. So they misinterpret normal fluctuations as spiritual setbacks. They assume progress should be linear. They expect forgiveness to feel settled all the time. And when it doesn't, they either push harder or give up.

Neither helps.

Forgiveness as a nervous system reset requires a different metric for success. Not "Do I ever feel triggered?" but "How quickly do I return to safety when I am?" Not "Do I remember what happened?" but "Does remembering it hijack me the way it used to?"

Healing shows up as shorter reactions, faster recovery, and less urgency.

Another reason forgiveness feels unstable is because many people try to forgive while their body is still dysregulated. They attempt to release while their system is flooded with adrenaline, fear, or anger.

That's like trying to learn a new language while your house is on fire. Regulation must come first.

Jesus modeled this, even if we don't always notice it. Before He healed, He often calmed. He touched. He reassured. He slowed people down. He restored dignity before demanding movement. He did not rush nervous systems past readiness.

Forgiveness works the same way.

You don't forgive *to* calm your body. You calm your body *so* forgiveness can take root.

This is where so many faith teachings accidentally reverse the order. People are told to forgive so they can have peace. But peace doesn't come from forcing forgiveness. Peace comes from **felt** safety, and felt safety allows forgiveness to settle.

That safety can't be faked. Your body knows the difference.

This is also why triggers are not the enemy. Triggers are information. They reveal where the nervous system is still holding tension, still scanning for threat, still waiting for reassurance. When approached with compassion instead of frustration, triggers become doorways to healing rather than proof of failure.

If forgiveness were an event, triggers wouldn't exist.
If forgiveness were an event, memory would disappear.
If forgiveness were an event, healing would be instant.

But forgiveness is a reset, and resets take time.

Another layer to this is repetition without retraumatization. Your nervous system needs repeated experiences of safety that do *not* reopen the wound. That means interrupting replays. Choosing silence over reaction. Grounding instead of spiraling. Each time you do this, you are teaching your system something new: *I can remember without being endangered.*

That lesson is powerful.

Over time, the nervous system learns that the memory does not equal threat. The charge softens. The reaction shortens. The urgency fades. And forgiveness, which once felt like effort, begins to feel like rest.

This is why the tools in this book matter. The Emergency Wallet Card. The Monthly Tracker. The grounding practices. They are not spiritual crutches. They are training tools. They support the nervous system while forgiveness matures.

Without tools, people rely on willpower.
Willpower burns out quickly.
Systems sustain healing.

Another reason forgiveness must reset the nervous system is because many offenses disrupted attachment. When attachment is threatened, the body goes into survival mode. Forgiveness alone does not restore attachment safety. Consistent regulation does. Boundaries do. Repeated experiences of being okay even when reminded do.

Your system needs evidence, not explanations.

This chapter is an invitation to stop measuring forgiveness by how calm you feel in ideal conditions and start measuring it by how well you recover in real ones. Forgiveness is not proven by the absence of reaction. It's proven by the presence of regulation.

You are not failing because your body still reacts. You are healing because it reacts less intensely than before. You are progressing because you recover faster than you used to.

That is what a reset looks like.

As you move forward, expect fluctuation. Expect moments of calm followed by unexpected triggers. Expect days where forgiveness feels effortless and days where it feels fragile. That's not regression, that's integration.

Forgiveness is settling in.

And in the next chapter, we will move from understanding the reset to practicing it intentionally, learning how to interrupt old patterns and establish new ones without forcing yourself to "be over it."

You are not late.
You are not broken.
You are not doing this wrong.

Your nervous system is learning a new language: safety.

And forgiveness is becoming something you live—not something you perform.

💊 Faith Prescription

Training the Nervous System to Stand Down

For this phase of treatment, your assignment is not to feel calm all the time. It is to practice returning to safety repeatedly. Forgiveness becomes stable when your nervous system learns that remembering does not equal danger. That learning happens through small, consistent resets, not one big emotional breakthrough.

This prescription invites you to focus on recovery speed, not reaction absence.

When you are triggered:

- Pause before responding

- Ground your body in the present moment

- Choose regulation over explanation

Say internally: *"I am remembering, not reliving. I am safe now."*

Each time you do this, you are retraining your nervous system. The work is subtle, but it is profound.

During this stage of treatment:

- Do not measure progress by how calm you feel

- Do not panic when triggers resurface

- Do not demand emotional perfection

Instead, celebrate quicker returns to baseline. That is forgiveness taking root.

<u>Prescription Duration</u>: Daily practice
<u>Reassessment</u>: After Chapter 9

🧬 Spiritual Vitamin: Truth That Builds Regulation

"Be anxious for nothing, but in everything, by prayer and supplication,
with thanksgiving, let your requests be made known to God.
And the peace of God, which surpasses all understanding,

will guard your hearts and minds in Christ Jesus."
— **Philippians 4:6–7**

Notice the order.

Request.
Release.
Peace that **guards**.

Peace here is not emotional suppression, it is protection. It guards what was once overwhelmed. And it does so *after* honesty, not instead of it.

Let this truth nourish you: peace is not something you force. It is something that arrives when the nervous system learns it no longer has to fight.

🕊 Holy Spirit Consult: Cooperation, Not Control

Sit quietly and place one hand on your body, wherever tension shows up most often. Then ask: ***"Holy Spirit, how can I partner with You to help my body feel safe right now?"***

You may sense:
- A slowing down
- A need to breathe
- An invitation to rest
- A nudge to stop explaining

Do not overthink the response. Regulation is often simple. The Holy Spirit works gently, not urgently.

🙏 Guided Prayer: Resetting Without Rushing

"God, I release the pressure to be instantly healed.
I release the fear that fluctuations mean failure.

Teach my body that it doesn't have to stay on guard.
Help me trust that safety can be learned again.

I receive Your peace, not as a demand,
but as a covering.

I allow forgiveness to settle
as my system learns rest.

Amen."

📝 Journal Reflection Page: Measuring The Right Things

Respond honestly. This page is about noticing progress you might otherwise miss.

1. When I am triggered now, I recover in:
   ☐ Seconds ☐ Minutes ☐ Hours ☐ Still varies

2. Compared to before, my reactions feel:
   ☐ Less intense ☐ Shorter ☐ More manageable ☐ Still unpredictable

3. One tool that helps my body calm is:

____

____

____

____

____

---

4. A moment recently where I chose regulation over reaction was:

---

5. One sentence I can practice is:
"Forgiveness is settling into my body, one reset at a time."

📖 Clinic Note: Read Before Proceeding

Forgiveness that reaches the nervous system
feels less like effort
and more like rest.

You are not retriggered because you're failing.
You are retriggered because your system is learning.

This chapter was not about mastering calm.
It was about cooperating with healing.

In the Faith Clinic, forgiveness is not proven by silence.
It is proven by resilience.

When you are ready, proceed to Chapter 9: ***Faith Clinic Treatment Plan: From Rehearsal to Release***

We will begin practicing forgiveness as a daily discipline: not through force, but through consistency.

Treatment is stabilizing.
Your body is learning peace.

Chapter 9

Faith Clinic Treatment Plan: From Rehearsal To Release

At some point in healing, awareness stops being enough.

You've noticed the replay.
You've named the attachment.
You've stopped minimizing the pain.
You've learned that forgiveness is a nervous system reset, not a one-time event.

And yet, without a plan, old patterns will quietly reassert themselves. This chapter exists because healing does not sustain itself on insight alone. Insight opens the door. Structure keeps you inside.

Rehearsal is not just a habit of thought; it is a conditioned response. It developed because your system needed a way to stay prepared, protected, and oriented after something disrupted your sense of safety. That response worked for a season. But now, it is costing you peace.

Release, therefore, cannot be passive. It must be *intentional*.

In the Faith Clinic, we treat healing the same way we treat physical recovery: with repetition, consistency, and realistic expectations. No one heals from surgery by understanding anatomy. They heal by following a rehabilitation plan. Forgiveness works the same way.

From this point forward, you are no longer just *observing* the pattern. You are **retraining** it.

The shift from rehearsal to release happens when the nervous system is given a new default response. Not an emergency override. A new baseline.

That baseline is interruption + regulation + redirection.

Most people try to jump straight to redirection, thinking positive thoughts, quoting scripture, distracting themselves. But without interruption and regulation first, redirection feels forced. It doesn't last. And when it fails, people assume they're broken.

They're not. They skipped steps.

Rehearsal begins automatically. Release must be practiced deliberately.

The first step is interruption, not suppression. Suppression shoves the thought down and creates pressure. Interruption acknowledges the thought and refuses to continue the loop. This is where many people get stuck because they think interruption requires willpower. It doesn't. It requires *permission*.

Permission to stop finishing the conversation.

You are not obligated to complete every thought that enters your mind. You are not required to solve a situation that has already ended. Interruption is the moment you recognize the replay and choose to disengage, not because the thought is wrong, but because it is no longer helpful.

Interruption sounds like:

- "This is the rehearsal."

- "I don't need to finish this."

- "This conversation is over."

That moment may last seconds. That's enough.

The second step is regulation. Once the replay is interrupted, your body still needs reassurance. Without regulation, the nervous system will pull you right back into the loop, searching for safety. This is where grounding becomes essential.

Regulation is not about calming down perfectly. It's about coming back into the present.

This may look like:

- Slowing your breath

- Dropping your shoulders

- Feeling your feet on the floor

- Naming what you see around you

- Placing a hand on your chest or stomach

These actions tell your body something your mind already knows: *I am not in danger right now.*

Only after regulation can redirection occur without force.

The third step is redirection, and this is where forgiveness begins to feel lived instead of labored. Redirection is not pretending the offense didn't matter. It's choosing where your attention goes next. It's allowing the present moment to take precedence over a past injury.

Redirection may be as simple as returning to what you were doing. It may be prayer. It may be silence. It may be choosing not to explain yourself internally. What matters is that the nervous system experiences a complete cycle: trigger → interruption → safety → forward movement.

That cycle, repeated consistently, is how rehearsal loses its grip.

Most people want release to happen through emotional catharsis. They want one big moment where it all lets go. While those moments can happen, they are not how most healing actually unfolds. Most healing happens quietly, through hundreds of small choices not to reenter the loop.

This is why treatment plans matter.

Without a plan, your system defaults to familiarity. With a plan, it learns something new.

Another critical part of this chapter is expectation management. Healing from rehearsal does not mean you will never think about the offense again. It means the thought no longer demands your participation. It becomes background noise instead of a command.

This distinction matters, because unrealistic expectations sabotage progress. If you believe healing means never remembering, every memory feels like failure. But if you understand healing means faster release, memories lose their power to discourage you.

The Faith Clinic measures progress differently.

We ask:

- Are you interrupting sooner?

- Are you regulating faster?

- Are you returning to the present more easily?

- Are you spending less time inside the loop?

If the answer is yes, even though it is inconsistent, you are healing.

Another key component of the treatment plan is compassionate consistency. Many people approach healing with intensity for a few days, then collapse under the pressure of perfection. They try to do everything "right," and when they can't maintain it, they quit.

Healing does not require intensity.
It requires gentleness applied consistently.

This means you will miss interruptions sometimes. You will catch the replay halfway through instead of at the beginning. You will have days where regulation feels harder. None of that disqualifies you.

Release is not a fragile achievement.
It is durable practice.

This chapter also addresses a subtle but important truth: rehearsals often resurface during growth. As you become more regulated, your system may feel safe enough to surface older material. This does not mean healing is reversing. It means capacity has increased.

Think of it as emotional unpacking. You don't empty the deepest boxes first. They come out when there's room.

The treatment plan is not about rushing to the end. It's about staying oriented when old patterns knock.

Another essential aspect of moving from rehearsal to release is identity shift. Rehearsal keeps you psychologically positioned as the one still inside the offense. Release shifts you into the present version of yourself, the one who survived, learned, and is no longer governed by that moment.

- ✓ Each interruption is an identity vote.
- ✓ Each regulation moment is a reminder: *I am not who I was then.*
- ✓ Each redirection reinforces a new truth: *This no longer gets to decide my internal world.*

Over time, the offense becomes information, not orientation.

You are not erasing the past.
You are reorganizing your present.

This chapter marks a turning point in the Faith Clinic journey. You are no longer just understanding unforgiveness. You are actively retraining your system toward peace. This is where forgiveness stops being theoretical and starts becoming embodied.

You may not feel dramatic relief yet. That's okay. Most progress feels anticlimactic at first. It shows up as slightly less urgency. Slightly more space. Slightly quicker returns to yourself.

That's release beginning.

As you move forward, remember you are not responsible for how the offense shaped you. But you are responsible for how much power it holds now. And power is reclaimed not through confrontation, but through consistent dis-engagement.

Rehearsal survives on attention.
Release grows through redirection.

In the Faith Clinic, we don't rush you to the finish line. We teach you how to walk without dragging the past behind you.

And in the next chapter, we will address one of the most misunderstood aspects of healing—how to forgive without reconciling, and why boundaries are not a failure of faith but a sign of it.

Treatment is active.
You are no longer rehearsing.
You are practicing release.

💊 Faith Prescription

The Interruption→Regulation→Redirection Protocol

For this stage of treatment, your assignment is not emotional perfection. It is pattern replacement. You are retraining your nervous system to move through a complete healing cycle every time rehearsal tries to take over. This is not about stopping thoughts, it is about refusing participation.

When rehearsal begins, follow this order:

1. **Interrupt**
   Name it without judgment.
   "This is the rehearsal."

2. **Regulate**
   Ground your body before moving forward.
   Breathe slowly. Drop your shoulders. Feel your feet.

3. **Re-direct**
   Return attention to the present moment.
   Choose not to explain, solve, or revisit.

Do not skip steps. Redirection without regulation will fail. Regulation without interruption will loop. The order matters.

During this phase of treatment:

- Practice the protocol even when it feels small

- Accept partial success as success

- Expect inconsistency without discouragement

Release is learned through repetition, not resolve.

Prescription Duration: Daily practice
Reassessment: After Chapter 10

🧬 Spiritual Vitamin: Truth That Reinforces Discipline

*"Do not conform to the pattern of this world,
but be transformed by the renewing of your mind."*
— **Romans 12:2**

Transformation here is not instant insight.
It is repatterning.

You are not suppressing thoughts, you are renewing pathways. Each interruption weakens the old pattern. Each redirection strengthens the new one. Let this truth nourish you: renewal is evidence of training, not strain.

🕊 Holy Spirit Consult: Strengthening The New Default

Sit quietly and ask: ***"Holy Spirit, where do I need more structure instead of more effort?"***

You may sense:

- A need for clearer boundaries around thought loops

- A reminder to slow down before reacting

- Permission to disengage without guilt

The Holy Spirit does not demand willpower. He supports consistency.

🙏 Guided Prayer: Choosing Practice Over Pressure

"God, I release the pressure to heal all at once. I choose steady practice instead of intensity.

Help me interrupt without arguing.
Help me regulate without forcing calm.
Help me redirect without explaining myself.

I trust that repetition will do
what willpower never could. Amen."

📝 Journal Reflection Page: Tracking What Actually Matters

Respond briefly. This is about noticing trends, not perfection.

1. I notice rehearsal most often when:

____

____

____

____

____

____

____

2. The step I tend to skip is:
☐ Interruption ☐ Regulation ☐ Redirection

3. When I complete all three steps, I feel:

____

____

____

____

____

4. One moment this week where I disengaged successfully was:

____

____

____

____

____

5. A sentence I will practice is: *"I do not need to participate in this loop."*

📖 Clinic Note: Read Before Proceeding

Release does not happen because you are strong.
It happens because you are consistent.

You are not undoing progress when rehearsals return.
You are strengthening it every time you disengage.

This chapter was not about dramatic freedom.
It was about quiet retraining.

In the Faith Clinic, forgiveness becomes sustainable when it is practiced, not pressured.

When you are ready, proceed to Chapter 10: *You Can Forgive Without Reconnecting*

We will clarify why boundaries are not bitterness, why reconciliation is optional, and why peace does not require access.

Treatment is stabilizing.
You are living forgiveness; one interruption at a time.

PERSONAL NOTES

____

____

____

____

____

____

____

____

____

____

Chapter 10

You Can Forgive
Without Reconnecting

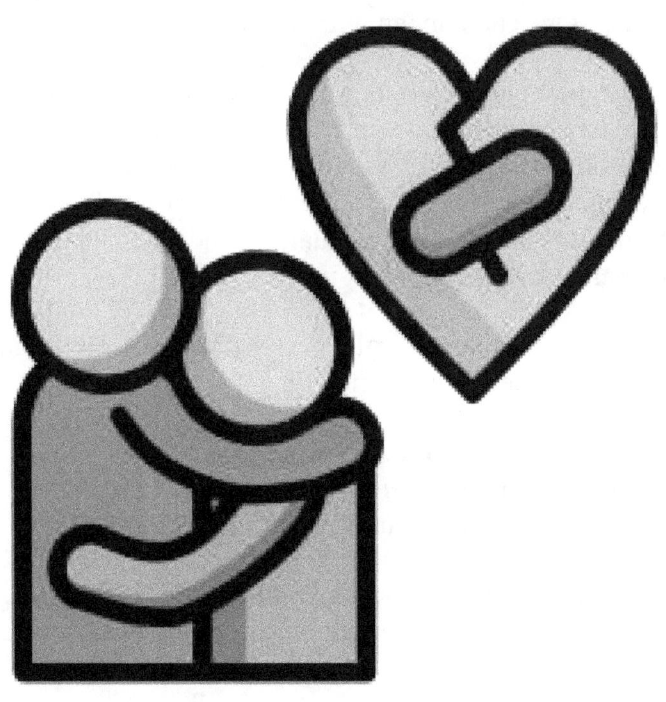

One of the most damaging lies people absorb about forgiveness is this: *if you've really forgiven, you should be willing to reconnect.* If peace is genuine, access should be restored. That boundaries are a sign of bitterness. That distance means you're still holding something against them.

This chapter exists to dismantle that lie completely.

 Forgiveness and reconciliation are not the same thing. They never have been. And confusing them has caused more harm than healing in faith spaces than we are willing to admit.

Forgiveness is an internal release. Reconnection is an external agreement. One can happen without the other, and often, it should.

Many people stay emotionally tethered to harmful situations because they believe forgiveness obligates them to proximity. They reopen doors God never asked them to reopen. They re-expose themselves to patterns that were never repaired. They silence their discernment to prove their spirituality. And when it hurts again, they blame themselves for "not forgiving enough."

But Jesus never equated forgiveness with access. He forgave freely, and He also withdrew strategically.

There were crowds He left.
Questions He didn't answer.
People He loved deeply but did not entrust Himself to.

Scripture says clearly that Jesus *"did not entrust Himself to them, for He knew what was in man."* That is not bitterness. That is discernment.

Forgiveness releases the debt.
Trust requires evidence.

Reconnection requires repentance, accountability, and change, not just words, not just time, not just spiritual language. And when those things are absent, distance is not a failure of love. It is an act of wisdom.

One of the reasons people struggle with this distinction is guilt. They fear that maintaining boundaries means they're disobeying God. They worry that they're unforgiving if they don't offer immediate access. They confuse kindness with availability. But forgiveness does not mean unlimited exposure.

Boundaries are not punishment.
They are protection.

Another reason reconnection feels mandatory is because people confuse peace with comfort, for others. They think if someone is uncomfortable with your boundary, it must be unloving. But peace is not the absence of tension. Peace is aligned with truth. And truth sometimes disrupts access.

You are not responsible for managing other people's feelings about your boundaries.

You are responsible for stewarding your healing.

In the Faith Clinic, we name this clearly: forgiveness is not proven by proximity. It is proven by freedom. If reconnecting destabilizes your nervous system, triggers old patterns, or reactivates harm, that is not forgiveness being tested, that is wisdom being ignored.

Another subtle trap is nostalgia. People reconnect not because the present is safe, but because the past was meaningful. They remember who the person *used to be*, who they *could have been*, or what the relationship *represented*. Nostalgia can masquerade as grace, but it often reopens wounds that were never repaired.

Forgiveness honors the truth of what was. Reconnection requires safety in what is.

This chapter is especially important for those who feel pressure, from family, church, or culture, to "keep the peace." Peacekeeping often demands silence, self-abandonment, and emotional compromise. But Jesus was never a peacekeeper. He was a peacemaker. And peacemaking sometimes meant walking away.

Forgiveness allowed Him to love without hatred. Distance allowed Him to stay aligned with purpose.

You are allowed to forgive someone and still say:

- "I don't trust you."

- "I don't feel safe."

- "I'm not available for this relationship."

- "Access is closed."

Those statements are not unchristian. They are honest.

Another misconception is that forgiveness requires explanation. That if you don't reconnect, you owe people a justification. You don't. Boundaries do not need footnotes. You are not obligated to relive your pain to make others comfortable with your healing.

Silence can be a boundary.
Distance can be holy.

Some people will accuse you of holding a grudge when you set boundaries. That accusation often reveals their discomfort with losing access, not your lack of forgiveness. Healing changes relational dynamics, and not everyone benefits from that change.

Forgiveness frees *you*.
Reconnection benefits *them*.

Those are not the same goal.

This chapter also invites you to examine where you may be using forgiveness language to override discernment. Saying "I've forgiven" should not mean "I'll tolerate harm." Forgiveness removes revenge from your heart, it does not remove your responsibility to protect yourself.

Jesus did not minimize wisdom in the name of mercy. He integrated both.

If you are wrestling with whether to reconnect, ask yourself:

- Has there been acknowledgment of harm?

- Has there been consistent change?

- Does my body feel safer now—or more alert?

- Am I considering reconnection from peace or from pressure?

Your body's response matters. Wisdom is not only cognitive, it is embodied.

Reconnection that comes from guilt will always cost you peace. Reconnection that comes from wisdom will feel grounded, slow, and mutual. And sometimes, the wisest choice is no reconnection at all.

That does not make forgiveness incomplete.

It makes it ***protected***.

This chapter is permission to stop confusing access with obedience. To stop sacrificing your nervous system on the altar of appearances. To stop reopening doors God may have closed for your safety.

You can forgive fully and still choose distance.
You can love without proximity.
You can release bitterness without restoring access.

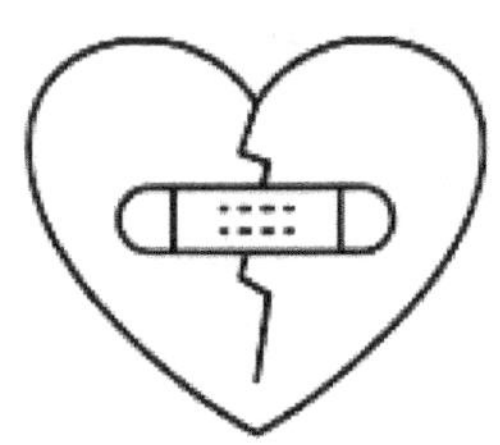

Forgiveness heals the past.
Boundaries protect the present.
Wisdom safeguards the future.

In the Faith Clinic, we do not measure healing by how much you tolerate. We measure it by how free you are to live aligned, regulated, and whole.

And in the next chapter, we will address what to do when others don't like your healing, and how to stand firm without hardening your heart.

You are not failing forgiveness.
You are practicing it wisely.

💊 Faith Prescription

Forgiveness Without Forced Access

For this phase of treatment, your assignment is not to explain your boundaries. It is to honor them without apology.

Forgiveness releases the debt.
Boundaries manage access.

This prescription invites you to stop equating reconciliation with righteousness. You are not required to reopen doors that compromise your peace to prove your faith. You are required to steward your healing wisely.

When guilt arises around distance, say internally:
"Forgiveness does not require proximity."

And let that be enough.

During this stage of treatment:

- Do not negotiate your boundaries with guilt

- Do not reopen access out of pressure

- Do not mistake discomfort for conviction

Boundaries are not rejection.
They are alignment.

Prescription Duration: As needed
Reassessment: After Chapter 11

Spiritual Vitamin: Truth That Protects Wisdom

"Above all else, guard your heart,
for everything you do flows from it."
— **Proverbs 4:23**

Guarding your heart is not withdrawal. It is discernment.

This verse does not command access, it commands stewardship. And stewardship means you decide what has permission to influence your inner life.

Let this truth nourish you: wisdom is not proven by how much you endure, but by how well you protect what God is healing.

🕊 Holy Spirit Consult: Discernment Without Fear

Sit quietly and ask: *"Holy Spirit, where am I feeling pressure to reconnect that You are not asking me to carry?"*

You may notice:

- Pressure from family expectations

- Pressure to appear forgiving

- Pressure to maintain peace at your expense

- Pressure to explain your healing

If pressure is present, pause. Conviction is gentle and clear. Pressure is urgent and heavy. God leads with peace, not coercion.

🙏 Guided Prayer: Choosing Wisdom Over Obligation

"God, I release the belief that forgiveness requires access. I release the fear of being misunderstood.

Help me stand firm without becoming hard. Help me love without reopening wounds. Help me trust that distance can be holy.

I forgive freely. I steward wisely.

Amen."

📝 Journal Reflection Page: Boundaries Without Shame

Respond honestly. This page is about clarity, not justification.

1. One boundary I feel guilty about is:

____

____

____

____

____

2. I feel pressure to reconnect because:

____

____

____

____

____

3. When I imagine reconnecting, my body feels:
☐ Calm ☐ Tense ☐ Alert ☐ Heavy ☐ Unsafe

4. Wisdom would sound like:

____

____

____

____

____

____

5. One sentence I can practice is:
"I can forgive fully and still choose distance."

Clinic Note: Read Before Proceeding

Forgiveness does not erase discernment.
It sharpens it.

You are not failing faith by choosing distance.
You are honoring healing by protecting peace.

This chapter was not about cutting people off.
It was about cutting guilt loose.

In the Faith Clinic, we do not confuse access with obedience or boundaries with bitterness.

When you are ready, proceed to Chapter 11: ***When People Don't Like Your Healing***

We will explore how to stay soft-hearted while standing firm, and how to respond without re-entering old patterns.

Treatment is stabilizing.
You are walking in forgiveness, with wisdom.

Chapter 11

Faith Prescription: Letting Go Without Losing Yourself

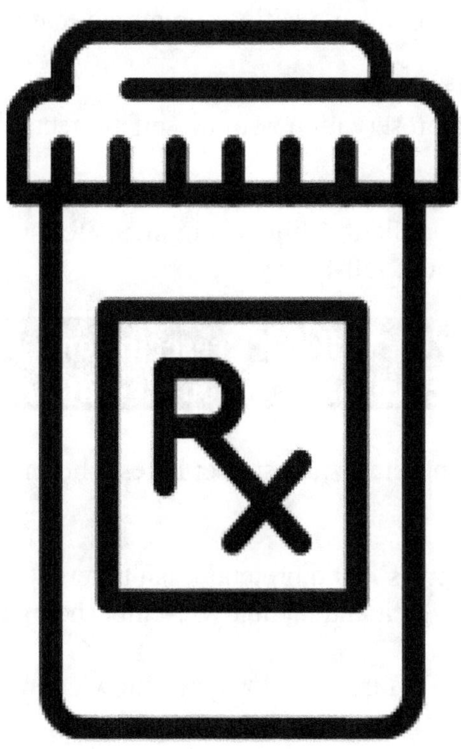

Letting go is often taught as if it requires self-erasure. As if release means shrinking, forgetting, excusing, or pretending something never shaped you. But true forgiveness, the kind that heals instead of hollows you out, does not require you to abandon yourself to prove obedience.

This chapter exists as a clinical stabilization chapter. Not to introduce new pain, but to teach you how to hold your ground internally when resentment resurfaces without re-entering the wound or hardening your heart.

Resentment does not mean you are failing.
It means your system is revisiting something that once mattered.

The goal here is not emotional perfection.
The goal is self-preservation without self-protection turning into isolation.

Below are the core Faith Clinic components for sustaining forgiveness without self-betrayal.

💊 Faith Prescription: What to Practice Daily When Resentment Resurfaces

When resentment returns, most people respond in one of two unhealthy ways:

1. They suppress it and pretend it isn't there.
2. They indulge it and mentally re-enter the offense.

This prescription offers a third way: acknowledgment without engagement.

Daily Practice:

- When resentment surfaces, pause.

- Name it neutrally: *"This is resentment resurfacing."*

- Do **not** ask why it's back.

- Do **not** analyze the offense.

- Do **not** correct yourself for feeling it.

Instead, follow this internal sequence:

1. **Acknowledge:**
   "Something in me is reacting."

2. **Reassure:**
   "I am safe now. I don't need to defend myself here."

3. **Release:**
   "I choose not to carry this forward today."

Resentment weakens when it is noticed without being fed.
You are not required to resolve it every time it appears.
You are only required not to ***merge with it***.

Practice this daily, not just when emotions are intense, but when they are subtle. Consistency matters more than intensity.

Spiritual Vitamin: Scriptural Truth That Stabilizes Emotional Healing

"Cast all your anxiety on Him because He cares for you."
— **1 Peter 5:7**

This verse does not say *manage, minimize,* or *justify* your emotional weight. It says cast: a physical, deliberate release.

Casting assumes weight existed.
It does not shame you for carrying it.

Let this truth stabilize you: God does not require you to be unaffected to be faithful. He invites you to transfer what is heavy, not deny it. Healing accelerates when you stop trying to carry what you were never meant to hold alone.

🕊 Holy Spirit Consult: Discernment Between Release And Avoidance

Sit quietly and ask this question without rushing the answer: *"Holy Spirit, am I releasing this, or avoiding it?"*

Then listen.

Release feels like:

- Softening

- Spaciousness

- Groundedness

- Relief without urgency

Avoidance feels like:

- Numbness

- Tightness

- Pressure to move on

- Irritation when it resurfaces

Neither answer is wrong. One simply tells you where care is still needed. The Holy Spirit does not rush you past what still requires gentleness. He does not confuse avoidance with obedience. Discernment brings clarity without condemnation.

🙏 Guided Prayer: Releasing the Offense Safely

"God, I don't want to hold onto this anymore, but I don't want to lose myself in the process.

When resentment returns, help me notice it without becoming it. Help me release without reopening wounds.

I give You the weight of this offense; not because it didn't matter, but because it no longer gets to lead me.

Teach me how to let go without disappearing, without hardening, without shrinking.

I choose freedom that preserves my wholeness.

Amen."

📝 Journal Reflection Page: Structured Prompts for Honest Processing

Write without censoring yourself. This page is not about resolutions, it's about clarity.

1. When resentment resurfaces, it usually sounds like:

____

____

____

2. The part of me that still feels affected is:

3. I'm afraid that letting go would cost me:

4. Letting go *without losing myself* would look like:

---

5. One sentence I can return to this week is:
"I can release the offense without abandoning myself."

📖 Clinic Note: Integration Reminder

Letting go does not mean becoming smaller.
It means becoming lighter.

You are not required to relive pain to prove forgiveness.
You are not required to forget to be free.
You are not required to reconcile to release.

This chapter is your reminder that healing can be contained, safe, and self-honoring.

In the Faith Clinic, forgiveness does not erase identity.
It restores it.

Treatment continues. You are doing this wisely.

PERSONAL NOTES

Chapter 12

Aftercare: When The Memory Comes Back, But The Power Doesn't

Healing doesn't end when the memory stops visiting. It ends when the memory no longer runs the house.

This chapter exists because many people mistake the return of memory for the return of failure. They think, *"If I were really healed, this wouldn't come back,"* or *"Why is this still here if I've forgiven?"* And in that moment, doubt tries to reclaim ground that healing has already taken.

Aftercare is where long-term freedom is protected. Not by erasing the past, but by removing its authority.

Memory Is Not the Enemy

The goal of forgiveness was never amnesia. God does not heal by deleting history. He heals by redeeming relationship to it.
Memory is how the mind stores experience.
Power is what the nervous system assigns to it.

Healing does not silence memory.
Healing unplugs memory from threat.

That's why a healed memory can surface without hijacking your body, your thoughts, or your day. You may remember what happened, but you don't relive it. You may feel a flicker, but it doesn't escalate. You may pause, but you don't spiral.

That is not relapse.
That is regulation.

This chapter normalizes something essential: memories can return without reopening wounds. The problem is not that memory shows up. The problem is when we panic and hand it the microphone.

The Difference Between Recall And Re-Entry

Aftercare begins with discernment.

Recall sounds like:
"That happened."

Re-entry sounds like:
"I'm back there again."

Recall is informational.
Re-entry is physiological.

If your body remains grounded, your breath steady, your awareness present, you are recalling, not reliving. And recall does not need intervention. It needs acknowledgment without engagement.

This is where many people unintentionally relapse. They feel the memory arrives and immediately start scanning themselves for symptoms: *Am I upset? Am I triggered? Am I failing?* That internal surveillance reactivates the nervous system and turns recall into re-entry.

Aftercare teaches you to respond differently.

When the memory comes back and the power doesn't, you do not interrogate it. You do not analyze it. You do not replay it to make sure it's "safe."

You let it pass like weather.

How To Respond When Old Feelings Resurface

Old feelings may still arise occasionally, not because healing is undone, but because your system is human.

The key is response, not reaction.

When an old feeling surfaces:

1. **Name Without Narrating**
   "This is an old feeling."

2. **Orient to the Present**
   Look around. Feel your body. Ground yourself where you are.

3. **Refuse the Spiral**
   Do not finish the story. Do not correct the past. Do not defend yourself internally.

4. **Return to Life**
   Continue with what you were doing.

That's it.

No processing marathon.
No emergency prayer session.
No internal argument.

You don't need to "fix" a feeling that is already losing its grip.

Aftercare is not about doing more work. It's about doing less when less is required.

Forgiveness Maintenance: A Sustainable Plan

Forgiveness does not need constant reinforcement, but it does need maintenance, just like physical health.

Here is your Faith Clinic Forgiveness Maintenance Plan:

Daily

- Interrupt rehearsals when they begin

- Practice grounding when needed

- Speak one self-honoring truth

Weekly

- Check in with your body (Where is tension living now?)

- Journal briefly without digging

- Reaffirm boundaries without guilt

Monthly

- Review progress (shorter reactions, faster recovery)

- Adjust tools as needed

- Release unrealistic expectations

Maintenance is not about vigilance.
It is about responsiveness.

You don't hover over healing.
You trust it and respond when necessary.

Relapse Prevention: Knowing The Difference Between A Signal And A Setback

Relapses don't look like memory returning.

Relapses look like:

- Rehearsing the offense again

- Questioning your worth again

- Reopening emotional access again

- Abandoning boundaries again

- Punishing yourself again

If you notice those patterns returning, do not panic. Relapse is not a verdict, it's a signal.

Signals don't mean you failed.
They mean something needs attention.

Return to basics.
Return to regulation.
Return to truth.

Healing does not collapse overnight. It drifts when neglected—and it stabilizes when supported.

Healing Removes Control, Not History

This is the truth that anchors everything:

You don't heal by forgetting.
You heal by reclaiming authority.

The memory may still exist.
The event may still matter.
The lesson may remain.

But it no longer dictates your emotional posture, your nervous system response, or your future decisions.

That's freedom.

If the memory comes back and the power doesn't, you're not stuck.

You're healed.

And healing that lasts is not loud, dramatic, or obvious. It's quiet. Steady. Unbothered by the past knocking on the door.

Because you finally changed the locks.

Aftercare Discharge Reminder

You are not responsible for never remembering.
You are responsible for not surrendering control.

Forgiveness didn't erase the memory.
It removed the grip.

And that is exactly how healing was always meant to work.

Faith Clinic Aftercare Complete.
Continue living. Healing will follow.

PERSONAL NOTES

152

Epilogue

This Is What Freedom Actually Looks Like

Freedom does not announce itself with fireworks. It doesn't arrive with a dramatic emotional release or a sudden erasure of the past. Real freedom shows up quietly, almost unnoticed at first, in the spaces where pain used to demand your attention and no longer does. It reveals itself in the moments when your mind starts down an old road and gently turns back without force. It settles in when your body remembers something painful and stays grounded anyway. This is the kind of freedom you have stepped into, subtle, steady, and real.

You came into this process carrying more than an offense. You carried the weight of unfinished conversations, emotional vigilance, spiritual pressure, and the belief that healing required perfection. You believed that forgiveness meant silence, that peace meant numbness, and that faith meant minimizing what hurt you. Along the way, those beliefs were dismantled, not violently, but truthfully. You learned that healing does not require you to disappear. It requires you to stay present.

This journey was never about becoming someone new. It was about recovering the parts of you that learned to hide, rehearse, or stay on guard in order to survive. You learned that those strategies were not failures of faith but intelligent responses to pain. And once they were honored instead of shamed, they no longer needed to run your life. Survival stepped aside. Safety took its place.

You now understand something many people never do: forgiveness is not a performance. It is a practice. It is lived out in how you respond, how you regulate, how you choose not to hand control back to what already ended. Forgiveness is no longer something you say to sound healed. It is something you do because you are healing. And because it is practiced, it is sustainable.

You are walking forward with discernment instead of defensiveness, with boundaries instead of bitterness, and with peace that does not depend on everything going right. You know the difference between remembering and reliving, between release and avoidance, between wisdom and fear. That knowledge is not theoretical anymore. It is embodied. It lives in how you breathe, how you pause, how you return to yourself.

There may still be moments when the past knocks. That is not a threat. It is a reminder of how far you've come. Each time it knocks and you do not answer with panic, explanation, or self-abandonment, you reinforce the truth: the past no longer has authority here. You are not fighting it. You are simply no longer governed by it.

This is what healing looks like when it lasts. It is calm, not chaotic. Grounded, not dramatic. Free, not fragile. It does not require constant effort, only honest attention. And it does not ask you to forget who you were, it allows you to live fully as who you are now.

You are not rehearsing anymore. You are not preparing for harm that has already passed. You are not waiting for peace to arrive before you live. You are living now, with clarity, with wisdom, and with your whole self-intact.

That is the victory.
That is the freedom.
And that is the life you are now free to keep living.

FINAL DISCHARGE SUMMARY:
You're Not Rehearsing Anymore. You're Living

This summary is not a slogan, a motivational close, or a moment of emotional hype. It is a clear, grounded acknowledgment of what has changed. You are being discharged not because nothing will ever surface again, but because what surfaces no longer controls you. Healing has taken place in the way that matters most: quietly, consistently, and sustainably. You are no longer organized around the offense. You are oriented toward your life.

Throughout this journey, you learned that healing does not require erasing memory. It requires removing authority. You stopped treating the past as something that needed to be solved repeatedly, explained endlessly, or rehearsed for protection. Instead, you learned how to be present without being invaded by what already ended. That shift alone marks real freedom. You are not healed because you forgot. You are healed because you remember without losing yourself.

You also learned that forgiveness is not proven by emotional perfection. You were never meant to feel calm every day, unaffected by reminders, or immune to human reaction. Healing was never about becoming emotionally flat or spiritually impressive. It was about developing capacity. You now recover faster. You return to yourself sooner. You notice patterns without obeying them. These are not small changes. These are the measurable signs of a regulated, healed nervous system.

Peace, as you discovered, is not a mood that stays forever. It is a practiced state. You no longer wait for peace to arrive before you live. You know how to practice it when emotions fluctuate, when memories surface, and when old feelings attempt to re-enter. Peace is no longer something you chase. It is something you maintain through awareness, boundaries, and self-trust. That means your peace is durable, not fragile.

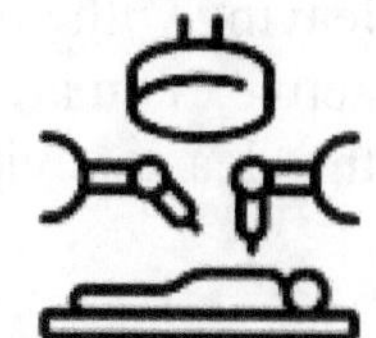

You are leaving this clinic with clarity instead of confusion. You understand the difference between recall and reliving, between release and avoidance, between forgiveness and forced access. You know how to interrupt mental rehearsal without shaming yourself. You know how to ground your body without rushing it. You know how to redirect your attention without denying truth. These are not theories anymore. They are skills you now possess.

It is important to say this clearly: you did not heal by becoming smaller, quieter, or less honest. You healed by becoming more anchored in yourself. You stopped abandoning your body, your discernment, and your boundaries in order to prove faith. You learned that forgiveness does not require self-erasure and that wisdom does not contradict love. You are now able to forgive without reconnecting, release without reopening, and remember without returning.

There may still be days when something unexpected surfaces. That does not revoke your healing. It confirms your humanity. The difference now is that you know what to do when it happens. You do not panic. You do not spiral. You do not hand control back to the past. You respond with regulation instead of reaction. You choose presence instead of rehearsal. That choice, repeated over time, is what healing looks like in real life.

You are officially discharged not because you no longer need care, but because you no longer need containment. You are no longer trapped inside old patterns, guilt-driven forgiveness, or fear-based protection. You can live forward while honoring what shaped you without being governed by it. The past may still exist, but it no longer directs your inner world or your future decisions.

This clinic did not change who you are. It restored access to who you already were before pain demanded survival strategies. You are leaving with yourself intact, your peace practiced, and your freedom active. You are not rehearsing anymore. You are living. And that is the clearest evidence of healing there is.

PERSONAL NOTES

🗓 FAITH CLINIC: FOLLOW-UP APPOINTMENT CARD

Because healing is maintained, not guessed.

Patient Name: ______________________________________

Diagnosis: Unforgiveness (Resolved / In Aftercare)

Treatment Track: Emotional Regulation + Forgiveness Maintenance

Provider: Faith Clinic — Inner Healing Unit

▦ Follow-Up Check-In

Recommended Review Window:
☐ 7 Days   ☐ 14 Days   ☐ 30 Days

Purpose of Follow-Up:
☑ Reinforce practiced forgiveness
☑ Assess emotional regulation progress
☑ Identify early signs of relapse (rehearsal, resentment, avoidance)
☑ Adjust boundaries and maintenance tools if needed

🩺 What to Check at Your Follow-Up

Use this card as your self-assessment reminder:

☐ Am I rehearsing less and living more?

☐ Do memories surface without hijacking my body?

☐ Is my recovery time shorter when emotions rise?

☐ Am I holding boundaries without guilt?

☐ Am I practicing peace instead of chasing it?

If most boxes are checked, treatment is holding.

🚨 Call for an Earlier Appointment If You Notice:

- Persistent mental rehearsal returning

- Emotional spirals lasting longer than usual

- Pressure to reconnect out of guilt

- Loss of grounding or increased reactivity

- Self-abandonment disguised as forgiveness

These are *signals,* not failures.

✍️ Provider's Notes / Adjustments:

____

____

____

____

🕊️ Reminder for the Patient

You are not coming back because you are broken.
You are checking in because you are **wise**.

Healing is not proven by never needing support.
It is proven by knowing **when** to use it.

Faith Clinic Status:
☑ Discharged — Stable
☑ Aftercare — Active
☑ Forgiveness — Maintained

Next Review: ________________________________

Keep this card somewhere visible.
Peace is practiced. You already know how.

PERSONAL NOTES

____

____

____

____

____

____

____

____

____

____

____

____

📑 FAITH CLINIC

DOCTOR'S ORDERS + 30-DAY FORGIVENESS TREATMENT PLAN

Edition: Unforgiveness
Attending Physician: The Holy Spirit
Patient Status: Stable but emotionally inflamed
Goal of Treatment: Release without denial. Peace without pretending.

📋 DOCTOR'S ORDERS (NON-NEGOTIABLE)

Effective Immediately, Patient Will:

1. **Cease all mental rehearsal** of unresolved conversations. (Replaying is not processing. It is reopening the wound.)

2. **Stop confusing forgiveness with access.** (Forgiveness releases *you*. It does not reinstate *them*.)

3. **Acknowledge emotional flare-ups without shame.** (Symptoms are data, not failure.)

4. **Practice nervous system regulation daily.** (Your body must learn what your faith already believes.)

5. **Speak honestly to God, not politely.** (Filtered prayers delay healing.)

6. **Refrain from forced reconciliation during treatment.** (No reopening wounds to prove maturity.)

7. **Follow the 30-Day Treatment Plan as prescribed.**
   (Skipping days does not cancel progress—but consistency accelerates it.)

Patient Initials: _________

Date Treatment Begins: _________

TREATMENT PHASES OVERVIEW

- **Days 1–7:** Awareness & Interruption

- **Days 8–14:** Emotional Release Without Re-Injury

- **Days 15–21:** Boundary Reinforcement & Identity Reset

- **Days 22–30:** Peace Conditioning & Aftercare Preparation

30-DAY FORGIVENESS TREATMENT PLAN

◇ DAYS 1–7: AWARENESS & INTERRUPTION

Objective: Stop automatic replay and name what's happening.

Daily Practice:

- Notice when the offense replays.

- Do *not* argue with the memory.

- Interrupt it gently and immediately.

Daily Declaration:

"I notice this, and I choose not to engage."

Daily Assignment:

- Write down:

    ○ What triggered the memory

    ○ What you felt in your body

    ○ What you wanted to say but didn't

(No fixing. No spiritualizing. Just noticing.)

Scriptural Stabilizer:

"Be still, and know that I am God." — Psalm 46:10

◇ DAYS 8–14: EMOTIONAL RELEASE WITHOUT RE-INJURY

Objective: Feel the pain without reopening the wound.

Daily Practice:

- Spend 5–10 minutes acknowledging what hurt.

- Do *not* re-explain or justify the story.

- Let the emotion rise and pass.

Guided Release Statement:

"This hurt mattered. I release it without rewriting it."

Daily Assignment:

- Journal one sentence:

    ○ "What hurt most was ________."

- ○ "What I needed then was ________."

(No conclusions. No closure yet.)

Scriptural Stabilizer:

"The Lord is close to the brokenhearted." — Psalm 34:18

◇ DAYS 15–21: BOUNDARY REINFORCEMENT & IDENTITY RESET

Objective: Separate your healing from their behavior.

Daily Practice:

- Practice saying internally:

  - ○ *"I forgive you, but I no longer carry you.*

Boundary Check-In:

- Ask yourself:

  - ○ Does this person have access to my peace?

  - ○ Am I confusing forgiveness with obligation?

Daily Assignment:

- Write one boundary you are allowed to keep.

- Affirm it without guilt.

Scriptural Stabilizer:

"Above all else, guard your heart." — Proverbs 4:23

◇ DAYS 22–30: PEACE CONDITIONING & AFTERCARE PREPARATION

Objective: Live without rehearsing.

Daily Practice:

- Replace replay with presence.

- Ground in current reality.

Peace Conditioning Statement:

"I am here. I am safe. I am not going back."

Daily Assignment:

- Each day, note:

    ○ One moment you *didn't* rehearse

    ○ One moment you chose silence over reaction

Progress is measured by **speed of recovery**, not absence of memory.

Scriptural Stabilizer:

"You will keep in perfect peace those whose minds are steadfast."
— Isaiah 26:3

⚠ RELAPSE NOTICE (READ IF SYMPTOMS RETURN)

Relapse does *not* mean treatment failed.
It means your nervous system is learning.

When symptoms return:

- Use your **Emergency Wallet Card**

- Repeat Doctor's Orders #1

- Resume the plan where you are, not where you "should be."

🕊 DISCHARGE READINESS INDICATORS

Patients are ready for discharge when:

- Memories arise without emotional hijack

- Silence feels safer than explanation

- Peace no longer depends on resolution

- Forgiveness feels like release, not effort

📝 FINAL CLINIC NOTE

You were never weak for holding on.
You are strong for learning how to let go.

Healing isn't forgetting.
It's remembering without bleeding.

🛏 FAITH CLINIC

MONTHLY FORGIVENESS
PROGRESS TRACKER

Edition: Unforgiveness

Edition: Unforgiveness
Tracking Period: _______________________________
Patient Name: _______________________________

Healing is not measured by how little you feel —
but by how quickly you recover.

WEEKLY OVERVIEW SNAPSHOT

Goal of This Tracker:
To identify patterns in emotional response, mental rehearsal, body regulation, and peace recovery — without shame or pressure.

1 WEEK 1: AWARENESS & INTERRUPTION
Primary Focus: Noticing without engaging
Check-In (Circle One Per Day)

Day	Replayed The Story?	Interrupted It?	Body Reaction	Recovery Time
Mon	Yes / No	Yes / No	Mild / Strong	Minutes / Hours
Tue	Yes / No	Yes / No	Mild / Strong	Minutes / Hours
Wed	Yes / No	Yes / No	Mild / Strong	Minutes / Hours
Thu	Yes / No	Yes / No	Mild / Strong	Minutes / Hours
Fri	Yes / No	Yes / No	Mild / Strong	Minutes / Hours
Sat	Yes / No	Yes / No	Mild / Strong	Minutes / Hours
Sun	Yes / No	Yes / No	Mild / Strong	Minutes / Hours

Weekly Reflection:

- What triggered me most this week?

- Did awareness increase, even if peace didn't yet?
  ☐ Yes ☐ No ☐ Unsure

🗓 WEEK 2: EMOTIONAL RELEASE WITHOUT REOPENING

Primary Focus: Feeling without rehearsing

Emotional Honesty Check

Day	Named the Feeling	Avoided Rehearsal	Allowed Emotion to Pass	Practiced Self-Compassion
Mon	Yes / No	Yes / No	Yes / No	Yes / No
Tue	Yes / No	Yes / No	Yes / No	Yes / No
Wed	Yes / No	Yes / No	Yes / No	Yes / No
Thu	Yes / No	Yes / No	Yes / No	Yes / No
Fri	Yes / No	Yes / No	Yes / No	Yes / No
Sat	Yes / No	Yes / No	Yes / No	Yes / No
Sun	Yes / No	Yes / No	Yes / No	Yes / No

Weekly Reflection:

- What emotion showed up the most?

- Did I judge myself for feeling it?
  ☐ Yes ☐ No

ⓘ WEEK 3: BOUNDARIES & IDENTITY RESET
Primary Focus: Forgiveness without access
Boundary Awareness Log

Day	Maintained Emotional Boundary	Felt Guilt For It	Reaffirmed My Right To Peace
Mon	Yes / No	Yes / No	Yes / No
Tue	Yes / No	Yes / No	Yes / No
Wed	Yes / No	Yes / No	Yes / No
Thu	Yes / No	Yes / No	Yes / No
Fri	Yes / No	Yes / No	Yes / No
Sat	Yes / No	Yes / No	Yes / No
Sun	Yes / No	Yes / No	Yes / No

Weekly Reflection:

- Where did I confuse forgiveness with obligation?

- Where did I choose myself without apologizing?

1 WEEK 4: PEACE CONDITIONING & RECOVERY SPEED

Primary Focus: Faster return to calm

Peace Recovery Tracking

Day	Trigger Occurred	Peace Returned Faster?	Used Tools (Wallet Card / Prayer)
Mon	Yes / No	Yes / No	Yes / No
Tue	Yes / No	Yes / No	Yes / No
Wed	Yes / No	Yes / No	Yes / No
Thu	Yes / No	Yes / No	Yes / No
Fri	Yes / No	Yes / No	Yes / No
Sat	Yes / No	Yes / No	Yes / No
Sun	Yes / No	Yes / No	Yes / No

Weekly Reflection:

- What helped peace return faster this week?

- What no longer had the same power over me?

NOTES:

____

____

____

📈 MONTHLY PATTERN REVIEW (MOST IMPORTANT SECTION)

Compared to the start of the month:

☐ I rehearse less

☐ I interrupt faster

☐ My body calms sooner

☐ I feel less urgency to explain

☐ I trust peace without closure

☐ I'm not fully healed, but I'm clearly freer

Biggest Shift I Notice:

Remaining Area God Is Healing:

📝 CLINIC NOTE: READ BEFORE TURNING THE PAGE

Healing does not mean the memory disappears.
It means it no longer controls your nervous system.

Progress is not silence.
Progress is recovery speed.

NOTES:

____

____

____

____

____

____

____

____

📟 FAITH CLINIC TOOLKIT

This toolkit exists because healing needs structure.
Feelings fluctuate. Systems stabilize.

📦 WHAT THIS TOOLKIT IS

The Faith Clinic Toolkit is a practical healing companion, designed to help the patient (reader) move from awareness to release without spiritual pressure or emotional denial.

This toolkit supports:

- Emotional regulation

- Honest forgiveness

- Boundary clarity

- Nervous system healing

- Long-term peace maintenance

📄 TOOL 1: FAITH CLINIC INTAKE FORM

Purpose: Diagnosis before treatment

Used When:

- At the beginning of the book

- When the reader realizes "I'm not as over this as I thought"

What It Does:

- Identifies the offense without minimizing it

- Separates pain from personality

- Exposes spiritual bypassing

- Establishes honesty as the foundation for healing

Print Instruction:

☐ Print once and complete fully

☐ Revisit only if symptoms significantly change

TOOL 2: FAITH CLINIC ID WRISTBAND

Purpose: Identity reinforcement during treatment

Used When:

- Emotional flare-ups

- Temptation to rehearse or reengage

- Pressure to forgive prematurely

What It Does:

- Reminds the patient they are "under treatment"

- Establishes non-negotiable truths about forgiveness

- Interrupts shame cycles

- Reinforces that healing is active, not passive

Print Instruction:

☐ Print on cardstock

☐ Cut and fold, or keep as a bookmark
☐ Read daily during treatment

🚨 TOOL 3: EMERGENCY WALLET CARD

Purpose: Crisis interruption

Used When:

- Triggered unexpectedly

- Emotional hijack begins

- Mental rehearsal starts looping

What It Does:

- Stops reaction before it becomes regression

- Grounds the nervous system

- Replaces replay with truth

- Provides a short, honest emergency prayer

Print Instruction:
☐ Print front/back
☐ Fold to wallet size
☐ Carry daily until symptoms reduce

📋 TOOL 4: DOCTOR'S ORDERS

Purpose: Authority + structure

Used When:

- The reader needs clarity instead of motivation

- Boundaries feel uncomfortable

- Healing feels slow

What It Does:

- Establishes clear expectations

- Removes guilt from the process

- Clarifies forgiveness vs. access

- Provides non-negotiable treatment guidelines

Print Instruction:
☐ Print and sign
☐ Post somewhere visible
☐ Refer back during resistance

📅 TOOL 5: 30-DAY FORGIVENESS TREATMENT PLAN

Purpose: Consistent healing over time

Used When:

- The reader is ready to stop rehearsing and start releasing

- Forgiveness feels overwhelming without structure

What It Does:

- Breaks healing into manageable phases

- Regulates the nervous system

- Rebuilds peace gradually

- Prevents emotional burnout

Print Instruction:
☐ Print full plan
☐ Follow daily without perfection
☐ Resume where you are if days are missed

⊞ TOOL 6: MONTHLY FORGIVENESS PROGRESS TRACKER

Purpose: Pattern recognition

Used When:

- The reader feels like "nothing is changing"

- Emotions lag behind obedience

What It Does:

- Measures progress by recovery speed

- Reveals growth that feelings hide

- Reduces self-judgment

- Confirms healing is happening

Print Instruction:
☐ Print monthly
☐ Complete weekly
☐ Review at the end of each month

🕊 TOOL 7: FINAL CLINIC TRUTH PAGE (INCLUDED)

You are not behind.
You are not failing.
You are not weak for needing structure.

You are healing correctly.

😬 HOW TO USE THIS TOOLKIT

Recommended Order:

1. Intake Form
2. ID Wristband
3. Doctor's Orders
4. 30-Day Treatment Plan
5. Emergency Wallet Card (carry daily)
6. Monthly Progress Tracker

Reminder:
This toolkit is not about speed.
It is about **sustainability**.

📝 FINAL NOTE FROM THE CLINIC

Forgiveness is not forgetting.
It is remembering without bleeding.

Peace is not passive.
It is practiced.

ABOUT THE AUTHOR

Dr. Patricia Tanner was born and raised in Sanford FL. She comes from a family of three siblings. Patricia Tanner is the founder of Multhai International Realty, Multhai Asset Management Services, and Multhai Investment Group which is located in Sanford, Florida. She is a graduate of the University of Central Florida, where she received a Bachelor of Science in Business Administration and a minor in Human Resources Management.

Dr. Tanner began her career shortly thereafter as a Regional Property Manager in the apartment community. Throughout her career in property management, she has built interpersonal relationships with corporate clients. She has a successful track record of increasing company revenues over $5 million annually, through hard work, commitment, creativeness, and strategic planning.

Her experience and leadership role eventually led her to achieve a Florida Real Estate Broker license. She spent fifteen years in the Real Estate field while completing a Master of Arts in Human Resources Management from Webster University, and a Master of Public Administration from Troy University. It was in this capacity that she decided to open her own brokerage company, Multhai International Realty.

In addition, Dr. Tanner finds time in her busy schedule to participate in her own Non-For-Profit Organization, Stones 2 Homes. She remains President of her organization in which she helps people build, keep, or purchase homes in affordable communities. She is the founder of PNT Property Partners in which she buys vacant land, develops it, and constructs brand new construction homes in Sanford Florida. Her overall goal is to educate and provide resources to help people overcome financial hardships and credit disadvantage to live the American Dream through homeownership in spite of economic hardship. Through her visions she will continue to grow as an entrepreneur and is willing to share her knowledge, experience, and expertise with anyone who is willing to learn.

MORE BOOKS BY THE AUTHOR

Welcome to the Faith Clinic—where your soul doesn't need to be perfect to be healed.

You've smiled through burnout. Quoted scripture while quietly unraveling. Prayed, fasted, and still felt like your faith flatlined. If that's you, Faith Clinic: Volume I is your spiritual prescription.

Dr. Patricia S. Tanner—known as The Faith Doctor—invites you into a raw, grace-filled recovery journey for the soul. With 7 powerful doses of faith-infused wisdom, this book delivers healing where performance failed and offers truth where church hurt left a scar. Designed especially for spiritually exhausted youth and young adults, each "dose" reads like an IV drip of hope for believers secretly running on empty.

You don't need to be okay to show up. You just need to be willing. The clinic is open.

NOW AVAILABLE:

www.amazon.com

Healing was just the beginning. Now it's time to grow.

If Faith Clinic Volume I met you in crisis, Volume II meets you in recovery. Because faith isn't a one-time fix—it's a lifestyle that needs maintenance, accountability, and consistency. Welcome to your follow-up care plan.

In Faith Clinic: Volume II, Dr. Patricia S. Tanner—aka The Faith Doctor—guides you through the next level of your spiritual healing journey. From navigating church trauma and burnout to facing silence from God and rediscovering purpose, this book goes deeper than devotionals. It's not about hype—it's about habits that sustain real, lasting transformation.

With raw wisdom, relatable stories, and no-shame truths, each chapter is a spiritual check-in for believers who want to thrive—not just survive. Whether you're wrestling with doubt, craving stability, or simply ready to grow up in God, this clinic is for you.

You've detoxed. Now it's time to build. Let's get you discharge-ready.

NOW AVAILABLE:

www.amazon.com

Welcome to the Faith Clinic: Anxiety Edition — where God doesn't coddle your coping mechanisms but confronts them with surgical precision.

This book is for the ones who love Jesus but still can't sleep. For the worship leaders crying in church bathrooms. For the believers who pray in spirals, fight shame on Sundays, and secretly think, "Maybe I'm the only one who can't seem to breathe through this." You're not crazy. You're just in a fight — and this book is your spiritual triage.

Inside you'll find:
- Panic attacks in pews and the prayers that still work.
- Scriptures that talk you off the ledge.
- What to do when you feel numb and God feels quiet.
- How to walk out of shame loops, judgment spirals, and performance religion.

This isn't just encouragement. It's equipment.
Because healing isn't a moment — it's a walk.

NOW AVAILABLE:

www.amazon.com

Welcome to the Faith Clinic: Stress Edition — where we don't hand you cute verses and clichés. We hand you spiritual prescriptions for real pressure, real panic, and real prayers from tired believers holding it together by a thread.

This book is for the overwhelmed—those trusting God while juggling bills, burnout, hustle culture, and holy frustration. If you've ever whispered, "God, are You even watching this mess?" this is for you.

Inside you'll find raw, soul-hitting chapters like:

- "God, I Trust You — But These Bills Keep Coming"

- "If Rest Is Holy, Why Does It Feel Like Slacking?"

- "I'm Tired of Smiling So You Won't Worry"

This isn't fluff. It's real talk for real stress—and a reminder that you're not forgotten, you're being fortified.

The Faith Clinic is open. Breathe in & take your spiritual vitamins. Healing begins here.

NOW AVAILABLE:
www.amazon.com

This isn't just a feeling — it's a flare signal from the soul. You pray, serve, and believe in God, but something deep inside is still simmering. Welcome to the Faith Clinic: Anger Edition — where suppressed emotions meet sacred intervention.

In this volume, Dr. Patricia S. Tanner guides you through spiritual triage for:

✅ Silent rage and emotional suppression

✅ The grief–anger connection

✅ Rejection wounds from childhood to church hurt

This isn't a lecture. It's a spiritual detox. No shame. No sugar-coating. Just raw, honest healing. Whether you're snapping at loved ones or silently seething under the surface, this book meets you at the boiling point—and leads you to the breakthrough.

🩺 This is the clinic.

🩸 This is your moment.

And God is ready to heal the anger behind your amen.

NOW AVAILABLE:

www.amazon.com

In this powerful installment of the Faith Clinic series, Dr. Patricia S. Tanner brings biblical insight, emotional compassion, and spiritual strength to those walking through grief. Designed as a healing chamber for the soul, each "dose" of this devotional targets a different dimension of sorrow—guiding you from pain to peace, from mourning to joy.

Inside, you'll discover:

- Daily doses of Scripture-based encouragement.
- Personal reflections and prayers for each stage of grief.
- Practical faith prescriptions to help you process loss and find purpose.

Whether you are navigating the recent loss of a loved one, confronting buried grief from the past, or supporting someone else in their sorrow, this devotional offers a gentle yet powerful roadmap to healing. Come, take your seat in the Faith Clinic—where the Great Physician is ready to restore your soul.

NOW AVAILABLE:

www.amazon.com

30 Days Of Grieving

Given By The Inspiration Of God

Healing From COVID-19

Almost a year later, it hit me... My mother was gone, and I was still stuck at the hospital. I had tried everything from crying to counseling, and even prayer. Pray they told me. Trust God they insisted. But it seemed as if nothing was working. I was hurt, dealing with my reality: my mother was not coming back.

While journeying through grief, it was under the divine 'Inspiration of God' that He placed me in a trance. While I was gaining a revelation about grief, He gave me this journal, '30 Days Of Grieving.'

NOW AVAILABLE:

www.amazon.com

The 30 Days Challenge:

I Tested POSITIVE for COVID-19

If you had 30 days to live, what would you do? If you were told that you needed to prepare for a marathon in 30 days and you were completely out of shape, what would you do first? If a family member handed you one million dollars and told you that you had to figure out how to build a house (debt free), how would you execute your plan?

I'm catching you off guard with these requests, right? Well, this is exactly what COVID-19 did when it snatched my mother's life away, wrecking my entire world. I had to battle for my mother AND my faith in 30 days flat. What a challenge!

Throughout this book, I will walk you through my brief journey with COVID-19, negative of a happy ending. I will share the diary I kept while attending to my mother, and the scriptures I read, prayed, and quoted as my shield and protection.

Take the journey with me, there is healing on the other side!

NOW AVAILABLE:

www.amazon.com

Can Salvation Get You Into Heaven? The Answer Is Yes! offers a powerful and biblically grounded exploration of God's eternal plan, revealing the heart of the Gospel and the assurance of salvation through Jesus Christ.

 Unpacking life's most vital questions—Who is God? Why were we created? What does Jesus' life mean for us?—this book brings clarity to the believer's journey and confirms that salvation, once received, is eternally secure.

Whether you're seeking understanding or affirming your faith, this inspiring guide will lead you into the confidence and joy of knowing heaven is your eternal home.

NOW AVAILABLE:

www.amazon.com

The Bench That Waited is a bold and prophetic call to action for believers who've grown comfortable in church attendance but stagnant in purpose.

With raw honesty and spiritual insight, Patricia Tanner exposes the quiet crisis of passive faith—where callings are delayed and obedience is optional.

Through Scripture, stories, and reflection, this book urges readers to rise from routine, break free from spiritual stagnation, and step boldly into their Kingdom assignment. The bench has waited long enough—will you?

NOW AVAILABLE:

www.amazon.com

What happens when the Kingdom becomes a stranger?

The Godless Climb is not a rejection of faith—it is a raw, unflinching journey through what remains when belief unravels. With brutal honesty and tender grace, this book explores the spiritual free fall that follows the loss of divine certainty, the ache of unanswered prayers, and the void left when God no longer feels near.

Written for those who have quietly slipped out of the pews and into a wilderness of doubt, grief, and inner searching, this is not a triumph story—but a survival story. A confession. A sacred wrestle. Through personal reflection and prophetic insight, the author unpacks what it means to climb without a safety net, to live without the scaffolding of religious performance, and to build a new compass in the absence of old crutches.

You haven't arrived. But you're still climbing. And that is holy.

NOW AVAILABLE:

www.amazon.com

The Triple 7 Formula is designed for business owners who are looking forward to hitting the million-dollar mark in their business. If you own a business and seem to be running in financial circles, this book will get you on track to simultaneously gaining sound business structure and millions in your bank account.

It was through many conversations with business owners lacking financial gain that prompted Patricia to share her blueprint for millionaire status. Through this book, she demonstrates how to gain financial ground by developing strong teams, implementing systems, and setting stackable goals. If you are ready to gain a laser sharp focus, and implement these clear steps, you will position yourself for financial greatness. Your business will be sound, and you will see financial growth beyond your wildest dreams!!

NOW AVAILABLE:

www.amazon.com

The Triple 7 Formula is specifically crafted for business owners aspiring to reach the million-dollar milestone. If you are a business owner feeling stuck in financial cycles, this book will set you on the path to building both a solid business structure and financial success.

This workbook is designed to complement the textbook of the same name. As you progress through its pages, you will be inspired to take decisive steps toward becoming a millionaire. From constructing your business framework to creating the millionaire's avatar, this process will expand your knowledge and mindset. Not only will you chart a course to financial success, but you will also identify your accountability circle and select a mentor to guide you toward greatness.

I cannot guarantee millionaire status unless you actively follow the steps to begin your journey. If you are searching for a get rich quick scheme, this workbook is not for you. I am looking for those ready to put in the effort—and since you are reading this, I believe that's you!

You have finally found it: Your roadmap to millions!

NOW AVAILABLE:
WWW.Amazon.com

Find Patricia on The Web:

www.PatriciaTanner.com

Follow Patricia on social media:

Facebook & Instagram: @PatriciaTannerInc